W9-CPM-810

GRAPHIC HISTORY

WINTER at VALLEY FORGE

by Matt Doeden

illustrated by Ron Frenz and Charles Barnett III

Consultant:

Wayne Bodle, PhD

Assistant Professor of History

Indiana University of Pennsylvania

Indiana, Pennsylvania

Capstone press

Mankato, Minnesota

Graphic Library is published by Capstone Press,
151 Good Counsel Drive, P.O. Box 669, Mankato, Minnesota 56002.
www.capstonepress.com

1 2 3 4 5 6 -10 09 08 07 06 05

Library of Congress Cataloging-in-Publication Data
Doeden, Matt.
    Winter at Valley Forge / by Matt Doeden; illustrated by Ron Frenz and Charles Barnett III.
    p. cm.—(Graphic library. Graphic history)
    Includes bibliographical references and index.
    ISBN 0-7368-4975-0 (hardcover)
    1. Washington, George, 1732–1799—Headquarters—Pennsylvania—Valley Forge—Juvenile
literature. 2. Valley Forge (Pa.)—History—18th century—Juvenile literature. 3. United States.
Continental Army—Military life—Juvenile literature. 4. Pennsylvania—History—Revolution,
1775-1783—Juvenile literature. 5. United States—History—Revolution, 1775–1783—Juvenile
literature. I. Barnett, Charles, III, ill. II. Frenz, Ron, ill. III. Title. IV. Series.
E234.D64 2006
973.3'341—dc22   2005010145

Summary:
In graphic novel format, tells the story of American patriot troops during the Revolutionary War
while wintering at Valley Forge, Pennsylvania.

Art and Editorial Direction
Jason Knudson and Blake A. Hoena

Designers
Bob Lentz and Juliette Peters

Colorist
Bill Anderson

Editor
Gillia Olson

Editor's note: Direct quotations from primary sources are indicated by a yellow background.

Direct quotations appear on the following pages:
Page 5, from *Journals of the Continental Congress, 1774–1789*, Library of Congress: American
    Memory, http://memory.loc.gov/cgi-bin/query/r?ammem/hlaw:@field(DOCID+@lit(jc00237))
Page 12, letter from George Washington to the State of New Hampshire, Dec. 29, 1777,
    (Gilder-Lehrman Collection document: http://www.pbs.org/georgewashington/collection/
    war_1777dec29.html)

TABLE OF CONTENTS

CHAPTER 1

THE ROAD TO VALLEY FORGE

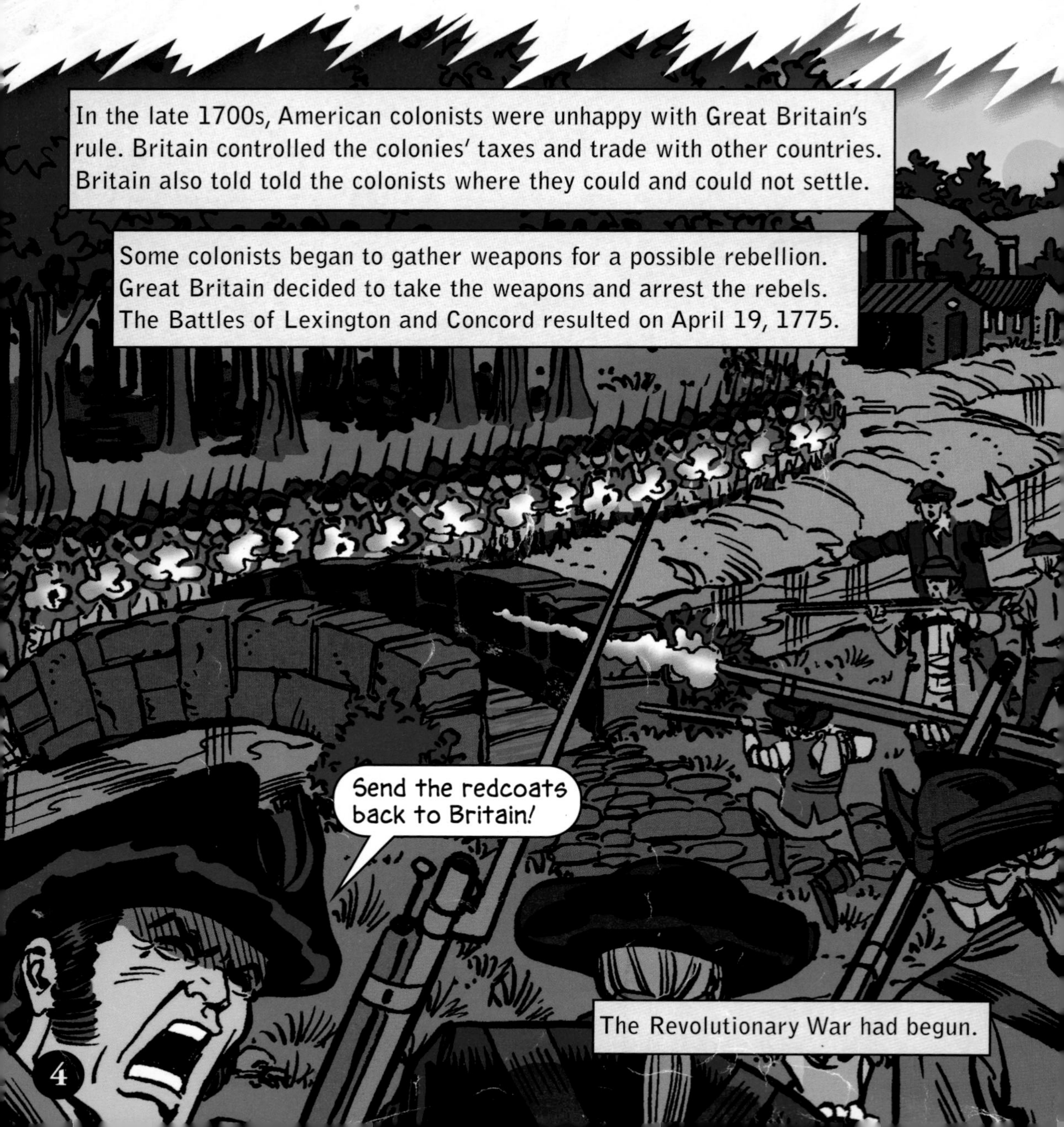
In the late 1700s, American colonists were unhappy with Great Britain's rule. Britain controlled the colonies' taxes and trade with other countries. Britain also told told the colonists where they could and could not settle.
Some colonists began to gather weapons for a possible rebellion. Great Britain decided to take the weapons and arrest the rebels. The Battles of Lexington and Concord resulted on April 19, 1775.
Send the redcoats back to Britain!
The Revolutionary War had begun.

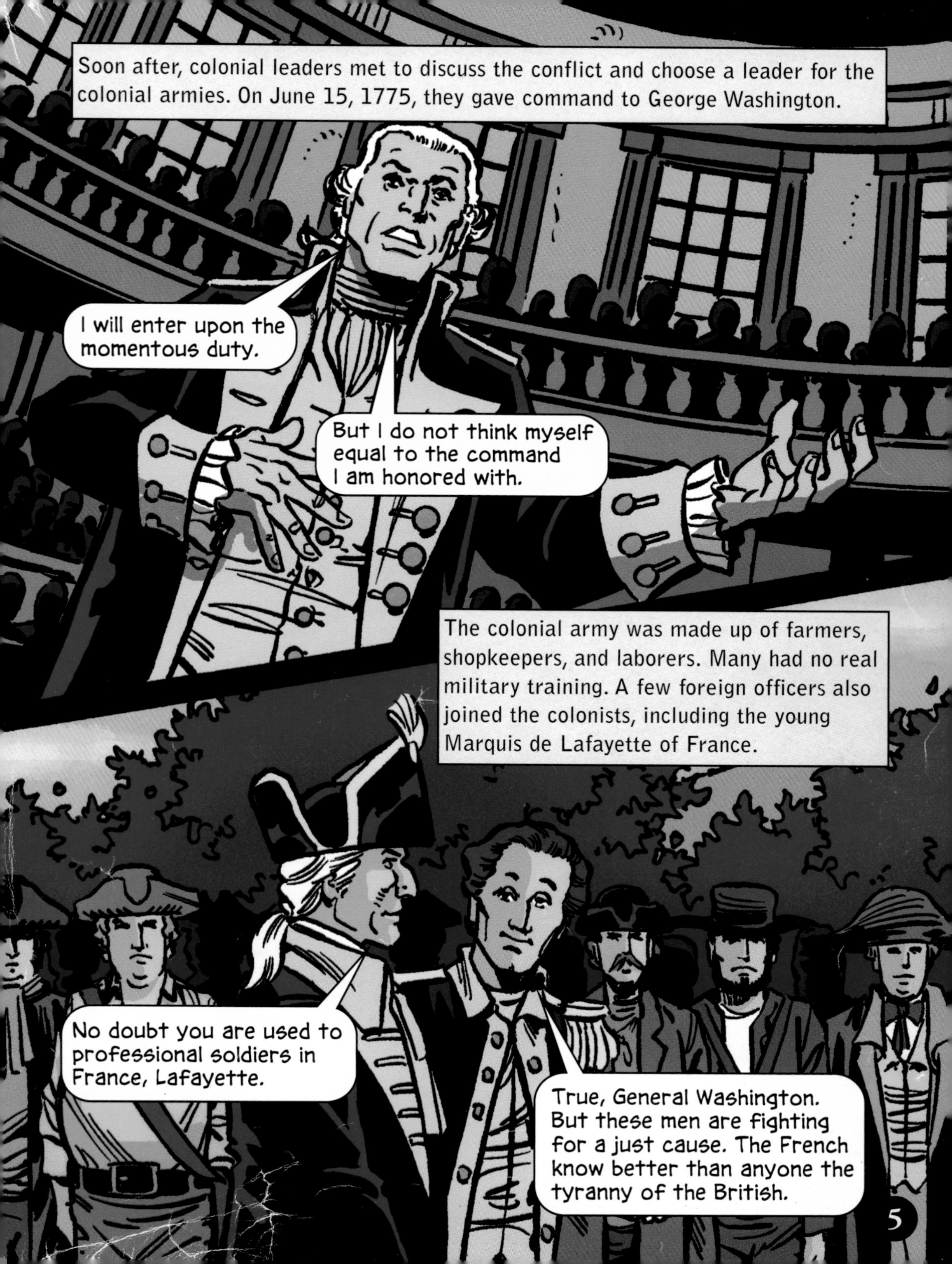
Soon after, colonial leaders met to discuss the conflict and choose a leader for the colonial armies. On June 15, 1775, they gave command to George Washington.
I will enter upon the momentous duty.
But I do not think myself equal to the command I am honored with.
The colonial army was made up of farmers, shopkeepers, and laborers. Many had no real military training. A few foreign officers also joined the colonists, including the young Marquis de Lafayette of France.
No doubt you are used to professional soldiers in France, Lafayette.
True, General Washington. But these men are fighting for a just cause. The French know better than anyone the tyranny of the British.

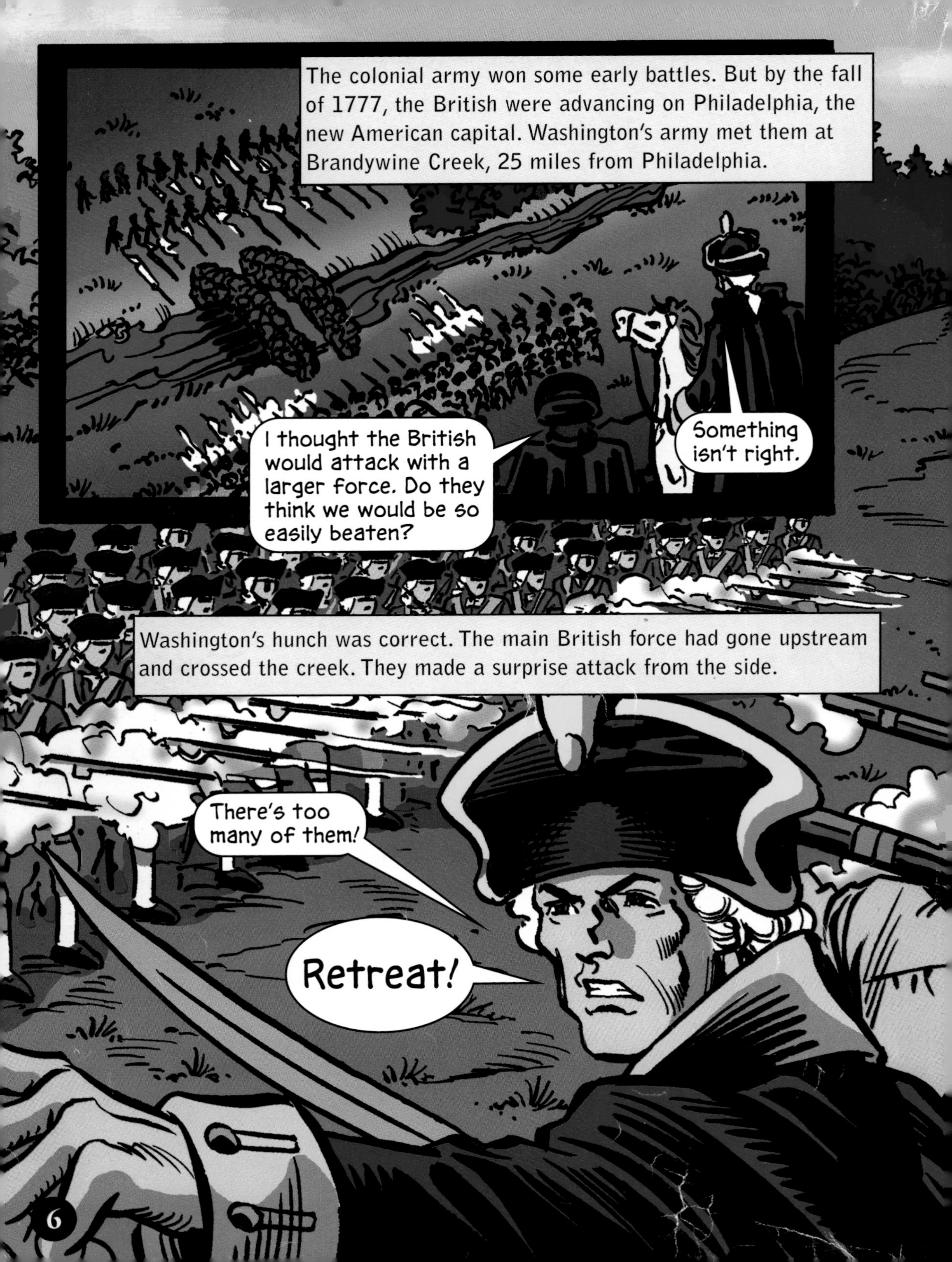
The colonial army won some early battles. But by the fall of 1777, the British were advancing on Philadelphia, the new American capital. Washington's army met them at Brandywine Creek, 25 miles from Philadelphia.
I thought the British would attack with a larger force. Do they think we would be so easily beaten?
Something isn't right.
Washington's hunch was correct. The main British force had gone upstream and crossed the creek. They made a surprise attack from the side.
There's too many of them!
Retreat!

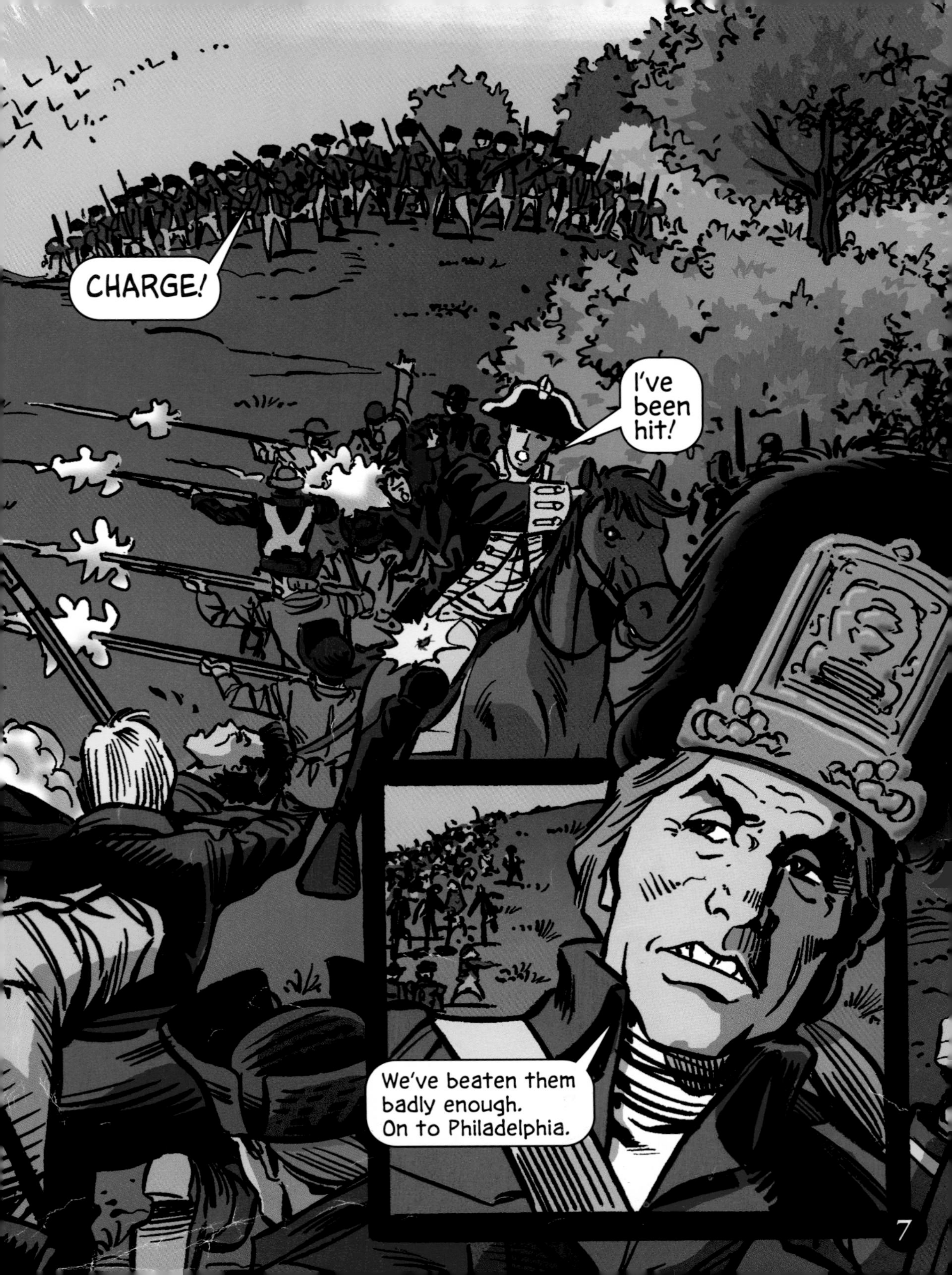
CHARGE!
I've been hit!
We've beaten them badly enough. On to Philadelphia.

CHAPTER 2

A NEW CAMP

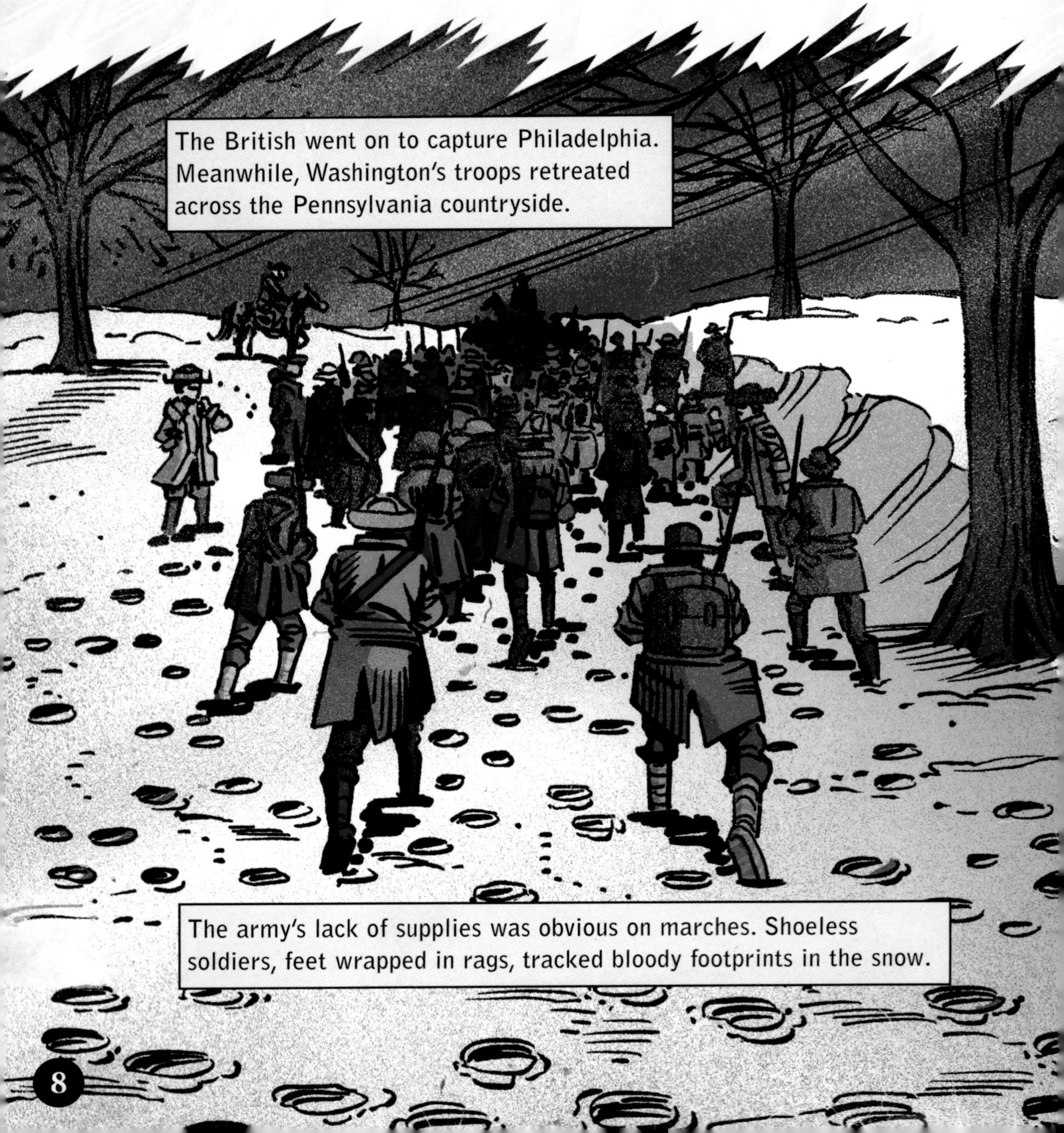
The British went on to capture Philadelphia. Meanwhile, Washington's troops retreated across the Pennsylvania countryside.
The army's lack of supplies was obvious on marches. Shoeless soldiers, feet wrapped in rags, tracked bloody footprints in the snow.

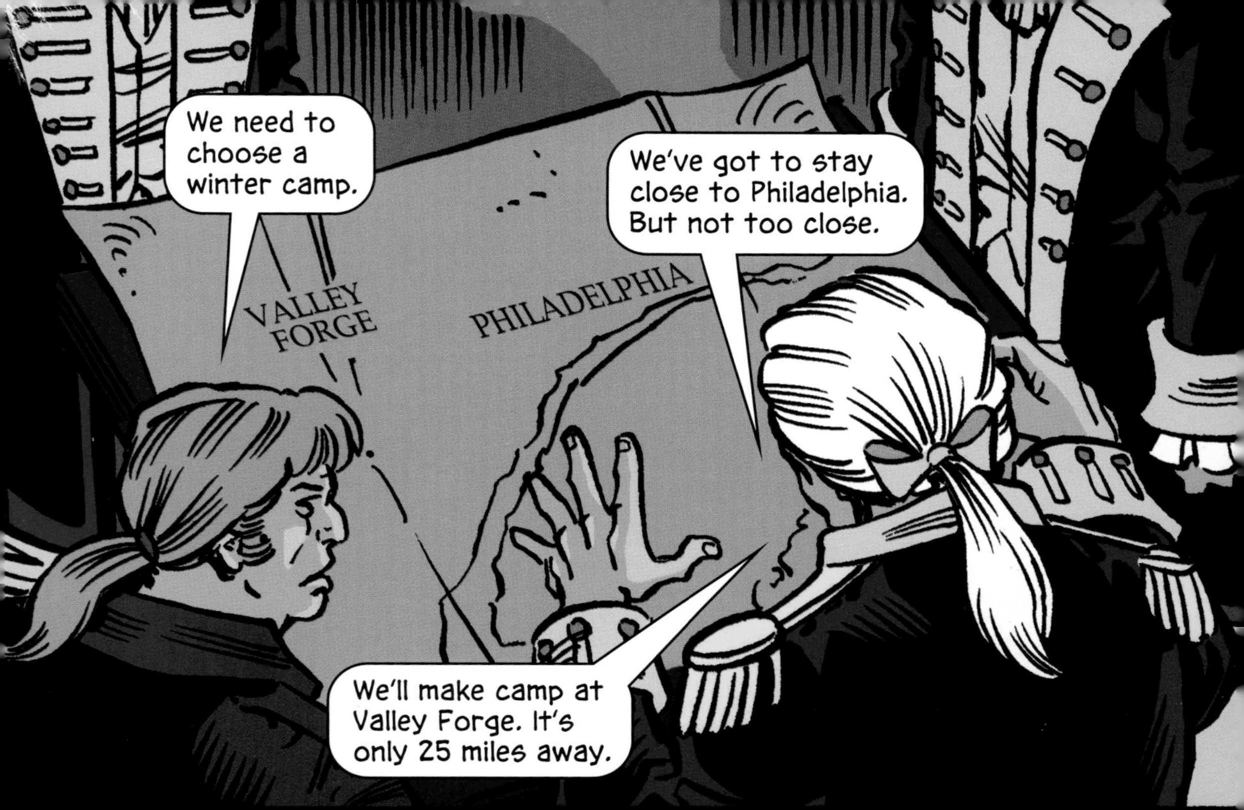
We need to choose a winter camp.
VALLEY FORGE
PHILADELPHIA
We've got to stay close to Philadelphia. But not too close.
We'll make camp at Valley Forge. It's only 25 miles away.

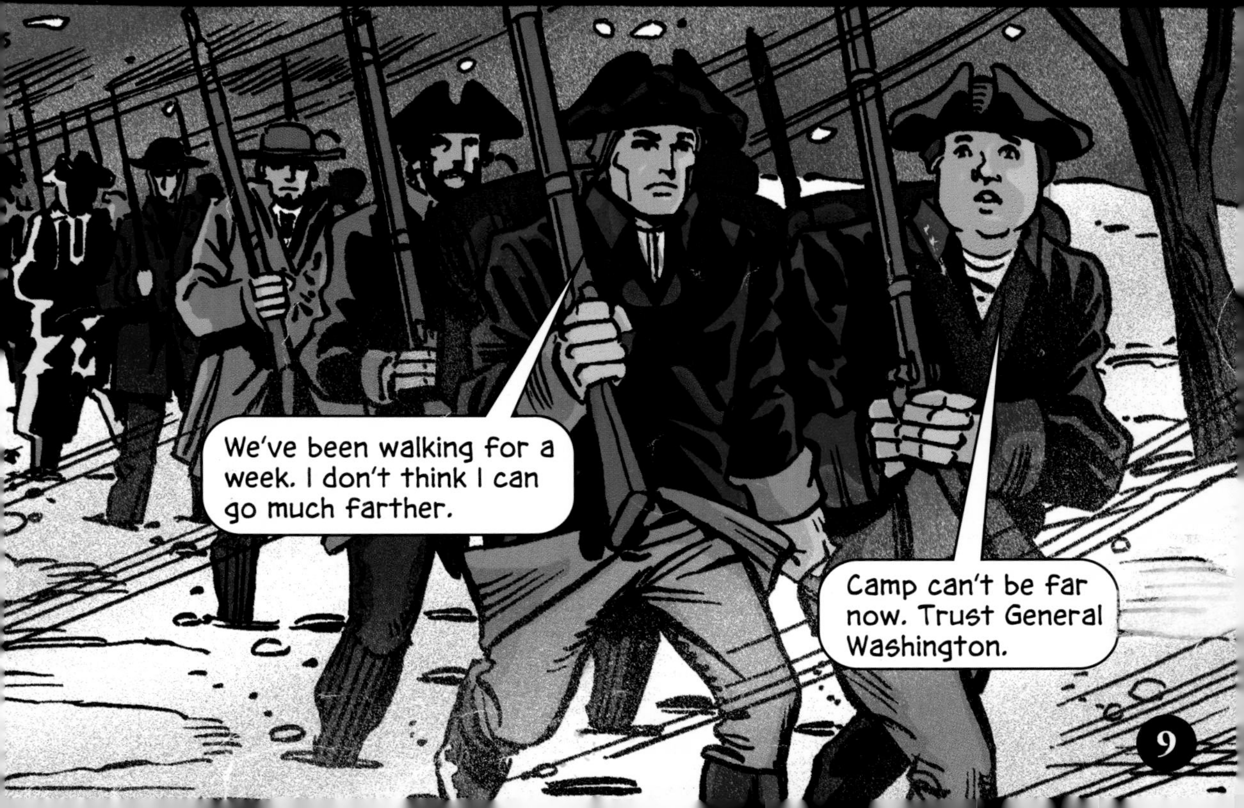
We've been walking for a week. I don't think I can go much farther.
Camp can't be far now. Trust General Washington.

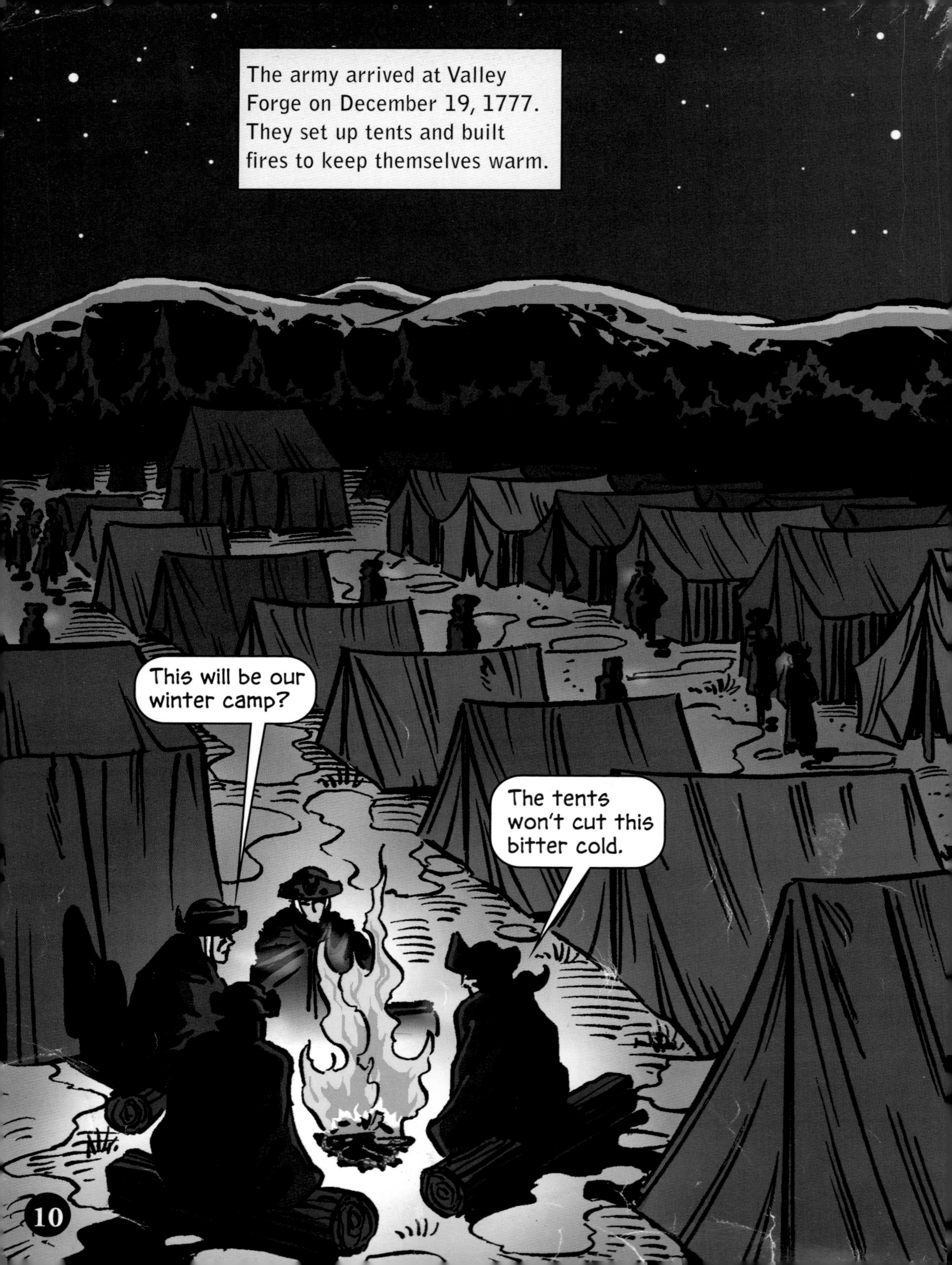
The army arrived at Valley Forge on December 19, 1777. They set up tents and built fires to keep themselves warm.
This will be our winter camp?
The tents won't cut this bitter cold.

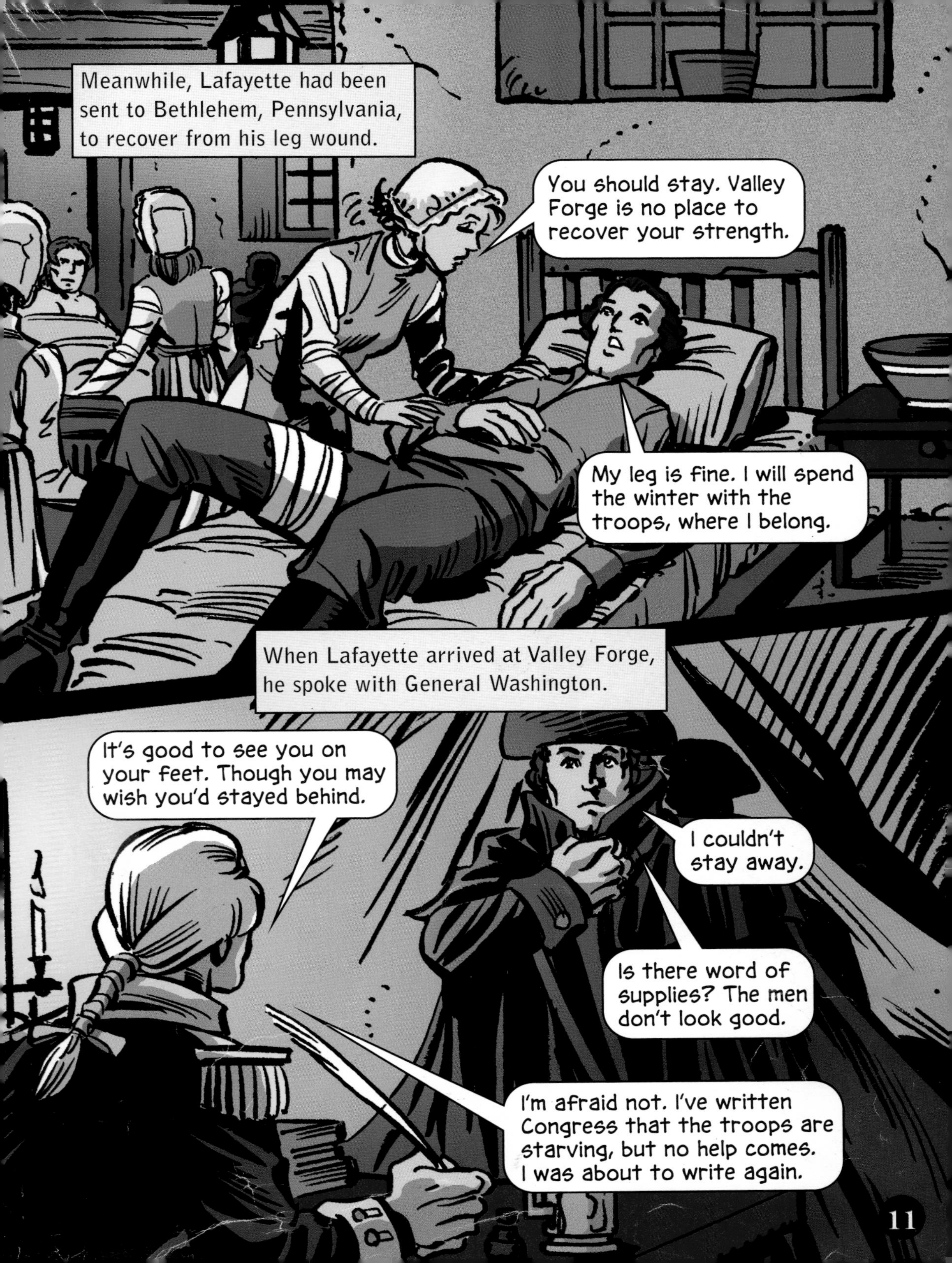
Meanwhile, Lafayette had been sent to Bethlehem, Pennsylvania, to recover from his leg wound.
You should stay. Valley Forge is no place to recover your strength.
My leg is fine. I will spend the winter with the troops, where I belong.
When Lafayette arrived at Valley Forge, he spoke with General Washington.
It's good to see you on your feet. Though you may wish you'd stayed behind.
I couldn't stay away.
Is there word of supplies? The men don't look good.
I'm afraid not. I've written Congress that the troops are starving, but no help comes. I was about to write again.

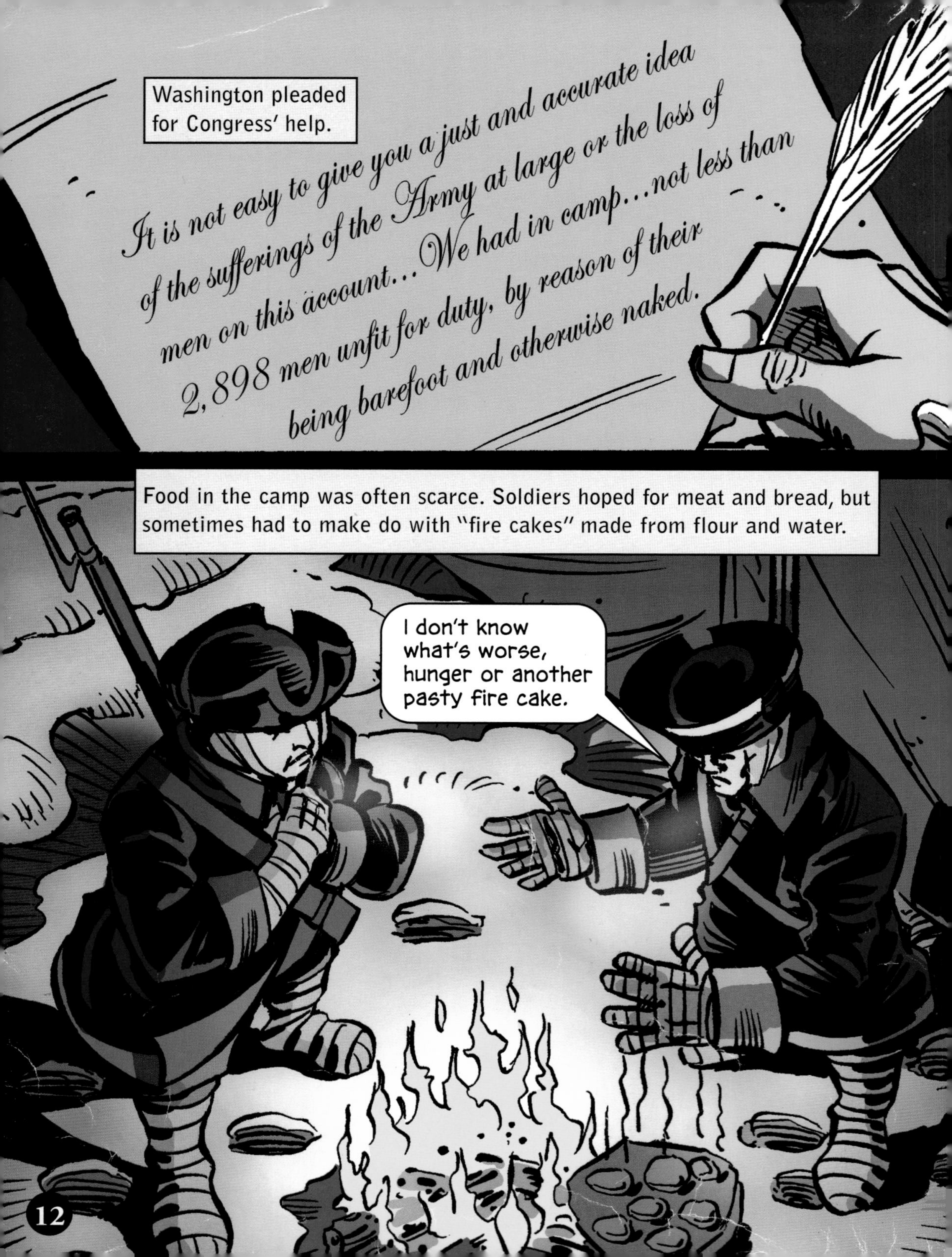
Washington pleaded for Congress' help.
It is not easy to give you a just and accurate idea of the sufferings of the Army at large or the loss of men on this account... We had in camp... not less than 2,898 men unfit for duty, by reason of their being barefoot and otherwise naked.
Food in the camp was often scarce. Soldiers hoped for meat and bread, but sometimes had to make do with "fire cakes" made from flour and water.
I don't know what's worse, hunger or another pasty fire cake.

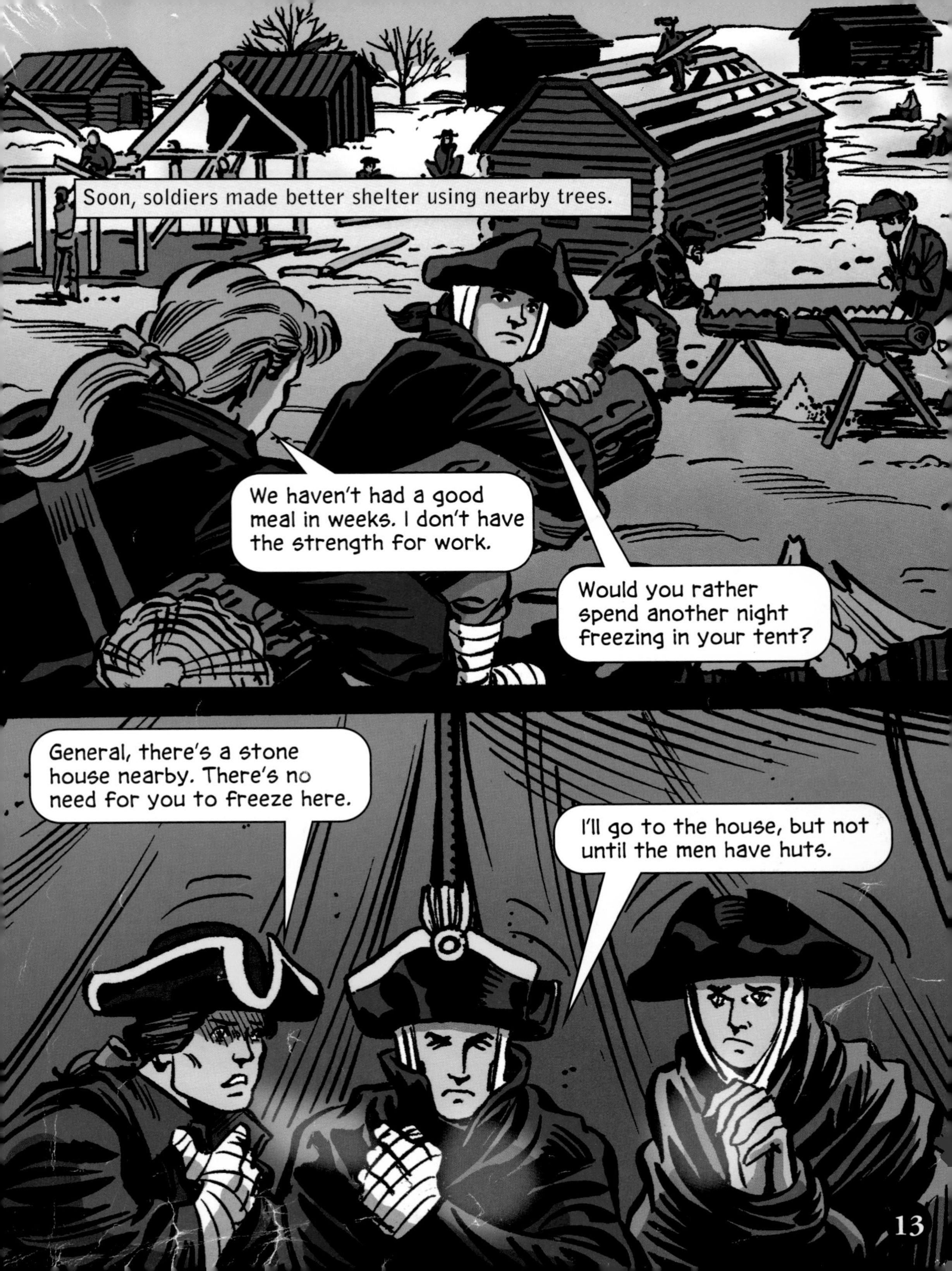
Soon, soldiers made better shelter using nearby trees.
We haven't had a good meal in weeks. I don't have the strength for work.
Would you rather spend another night freezing in your tent?
General, there's a stone house nearby. There's no need for you to freeze here.
I'll go to the house, but not until the men have huts.

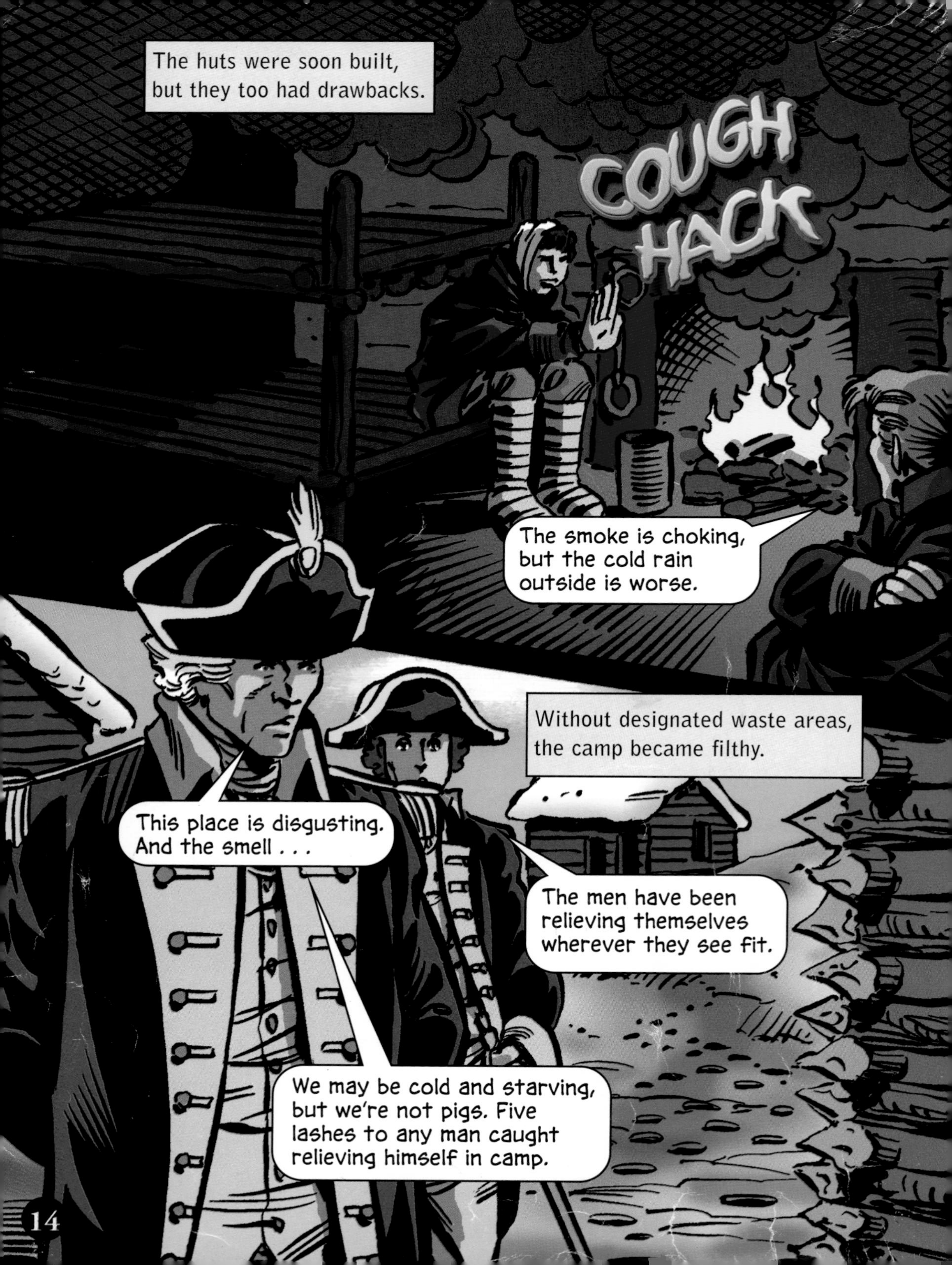

The huts were soon built, but they too had drawbacks.
COUGH HACK
The smoke is choking, but the cold rain outside is worse.
Without designated waste areas, the camp became filthy.
This place is disgusting. And the smell . . .
The men have been relieving themselves wherever they see fit.
We may be cold and starving, but we're not pigs. Five lashes to any man caught relieving himself in camp.

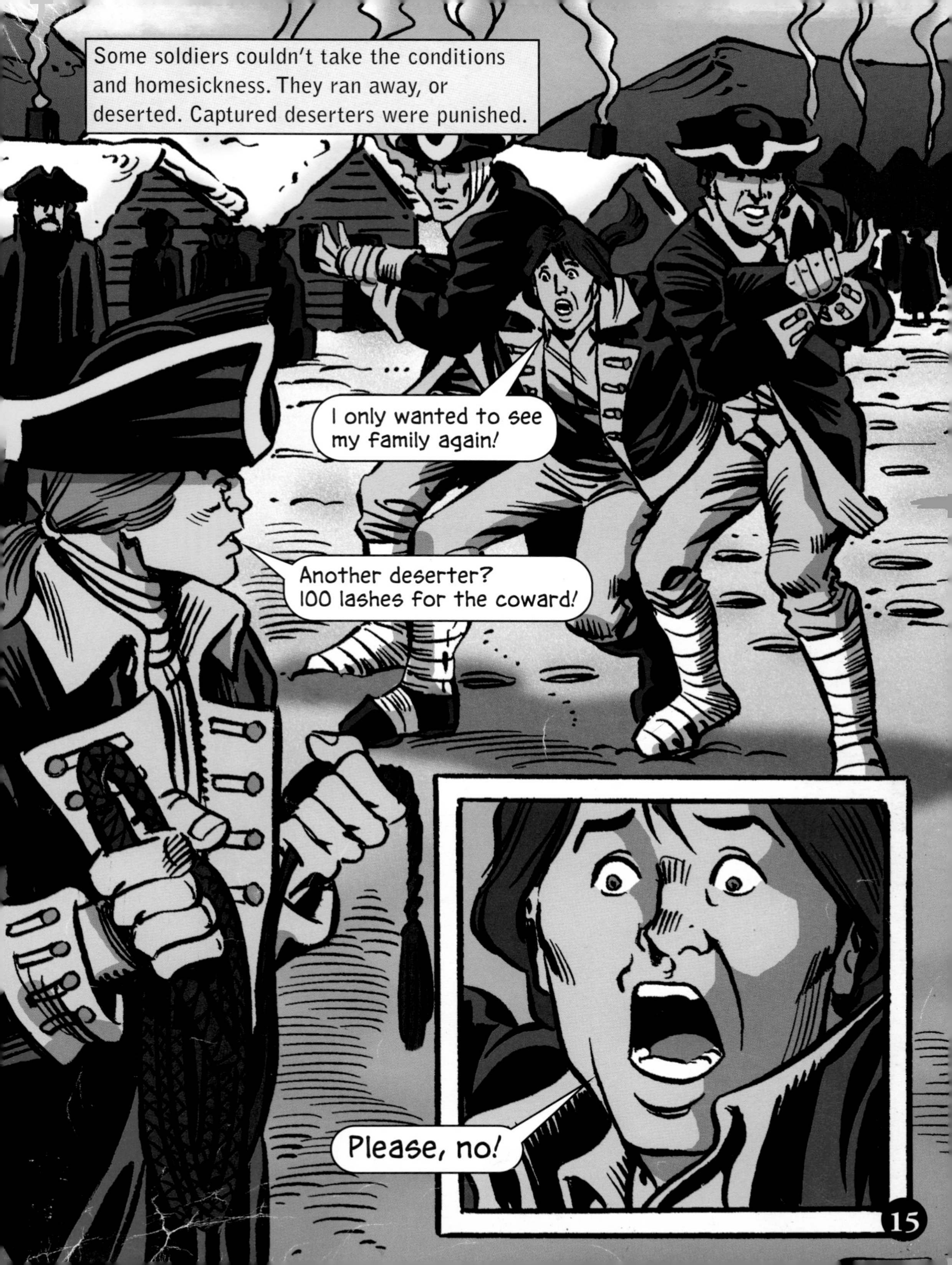
Some soldiers couldn't take the conditions and homesickness. They ran away, or deserted. Captured deserters were punished.
I only wanted to see my family again!
Another deserter? 100 lashes for the coward!
Please, no!

CHAPTER 3

THE LONG WINTER

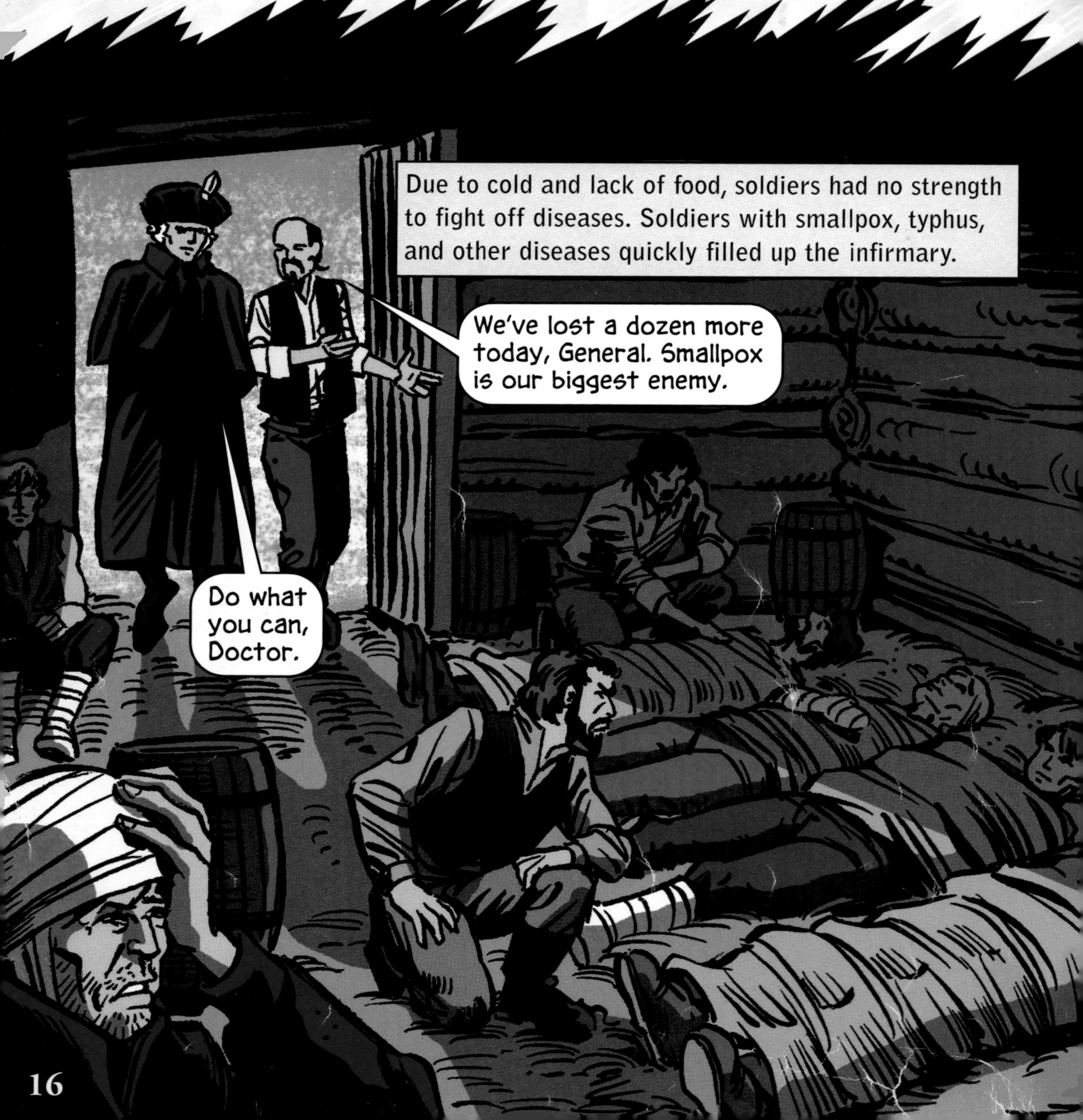

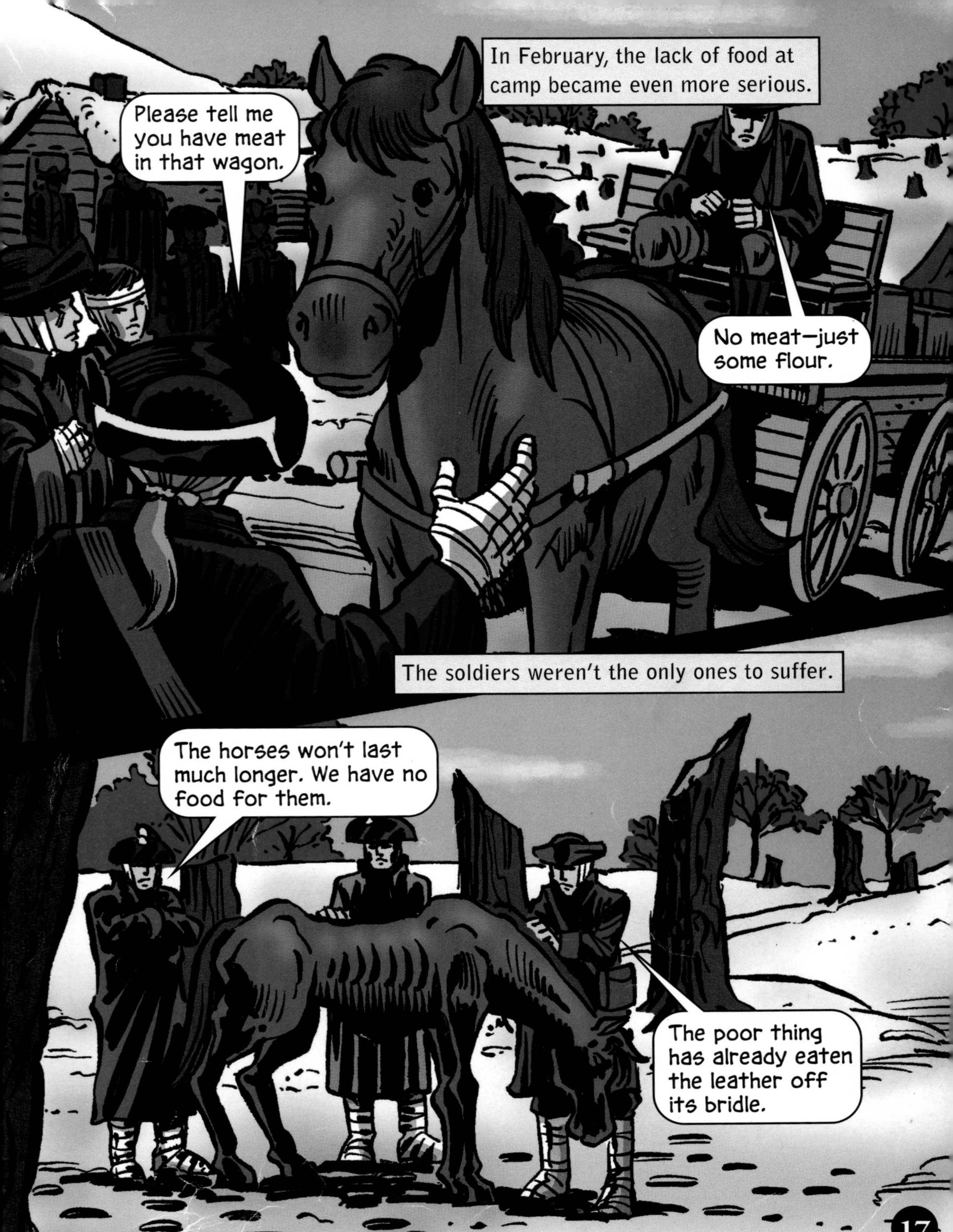
In February, the lack of food at camp became even more serious.
Please tell me you have meat in that wagon.
No meat—just some flour.
The soldiers weren't the only ones to suffer.
The horses won't last much longer. We have no food for them.
The poor thing has already eaten the leather off its bridle.

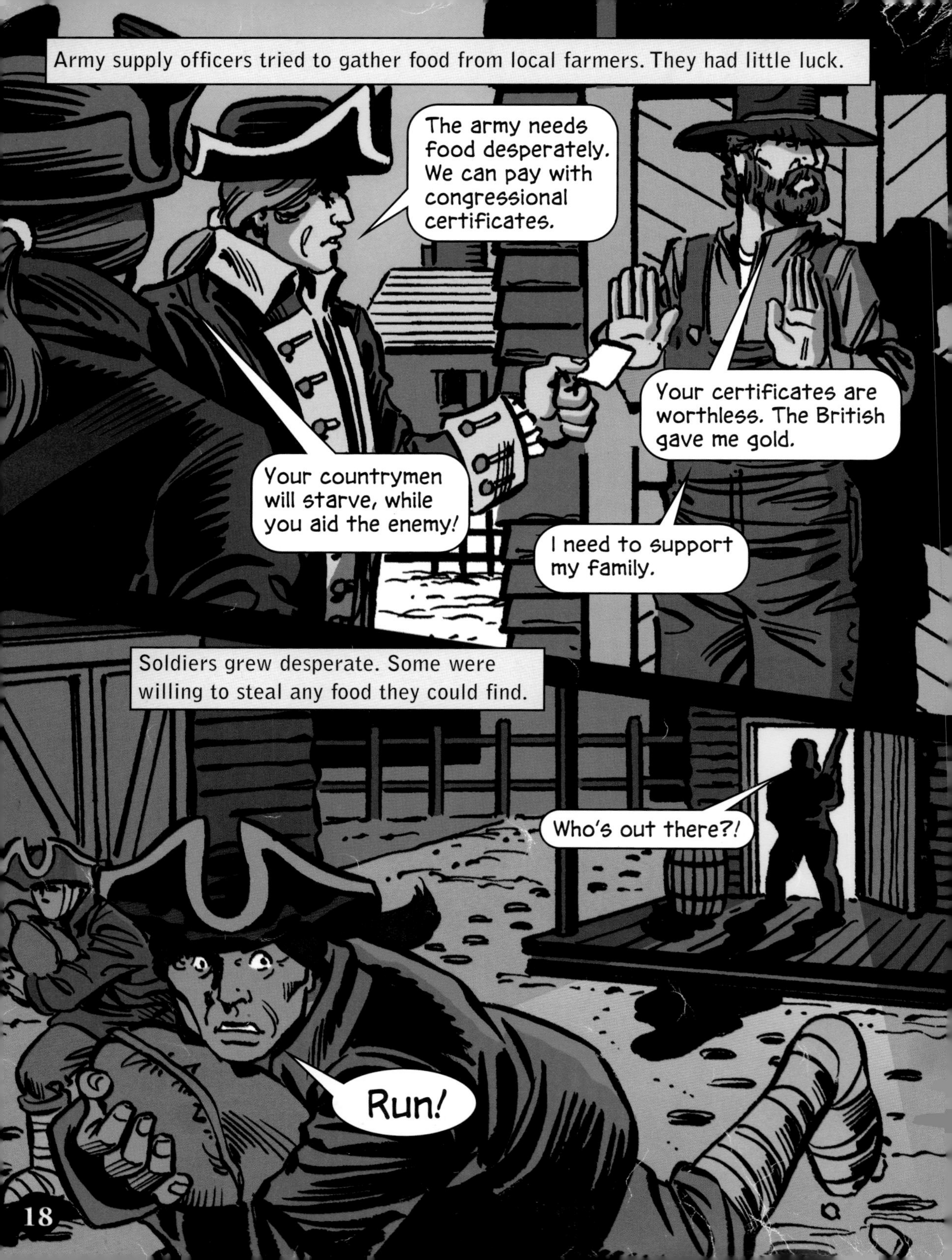
Army supply officers tried to gather food from local farmers. They had little luck.
The army needs food desperately. We can pay with congressional certificates.
Your certificates are worthless. The British gave me gold.
Your countrymen will starve, while you aid the enemy!
I need to support my family.
Soldiers grew desperate. Some were willing to steal any food they could find.
Who's out there?!
Run!

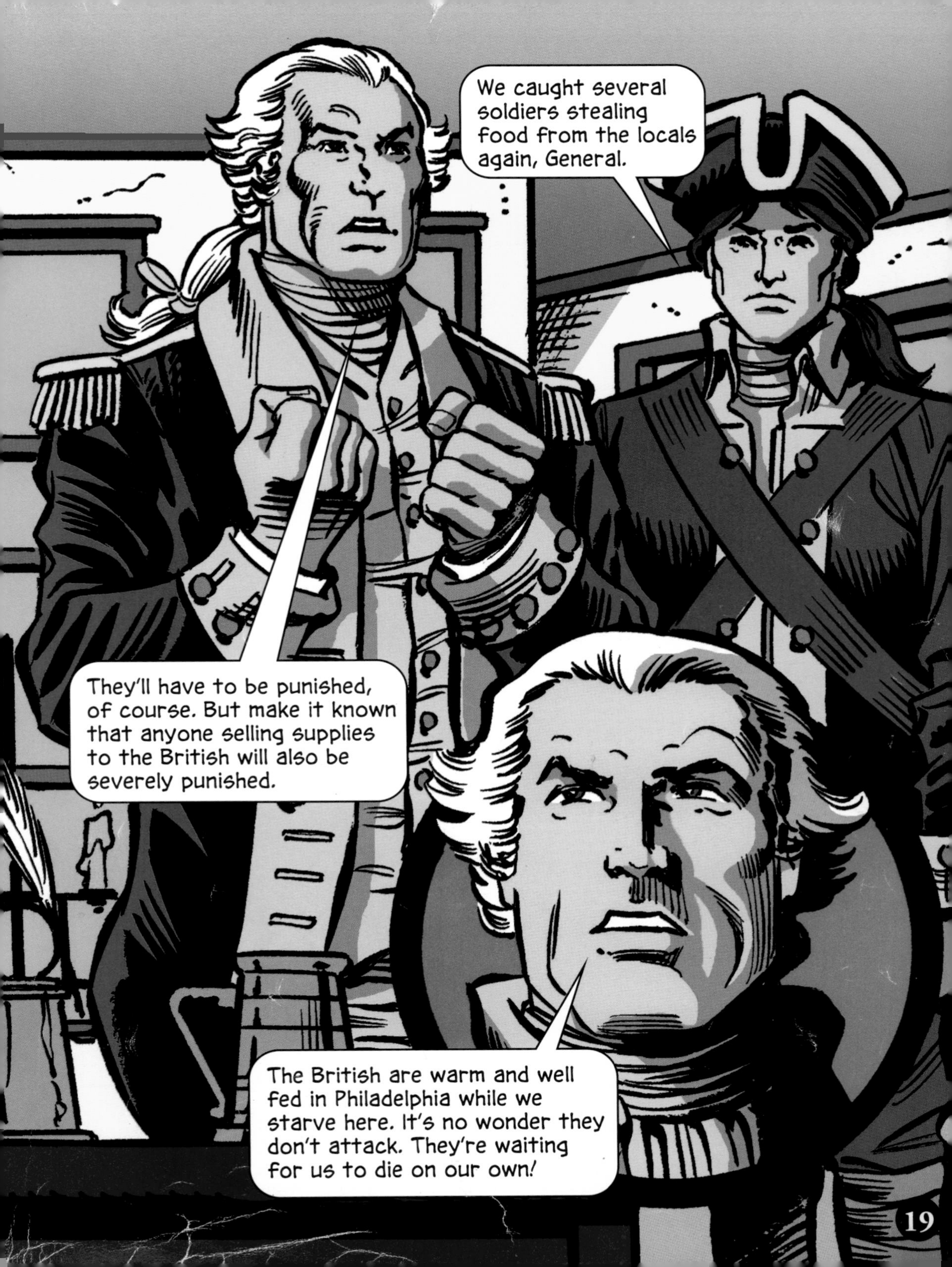
We caught several soldiers stealing food from the locals again, General.
They'll have to be punished, of course. But make it known that anyone selling supplies to the British will also be severely punished.
The British are warm and well fed in Philadelphia while we starve here. It's no wonder they don't attack. They're waiting for us to die on our own!

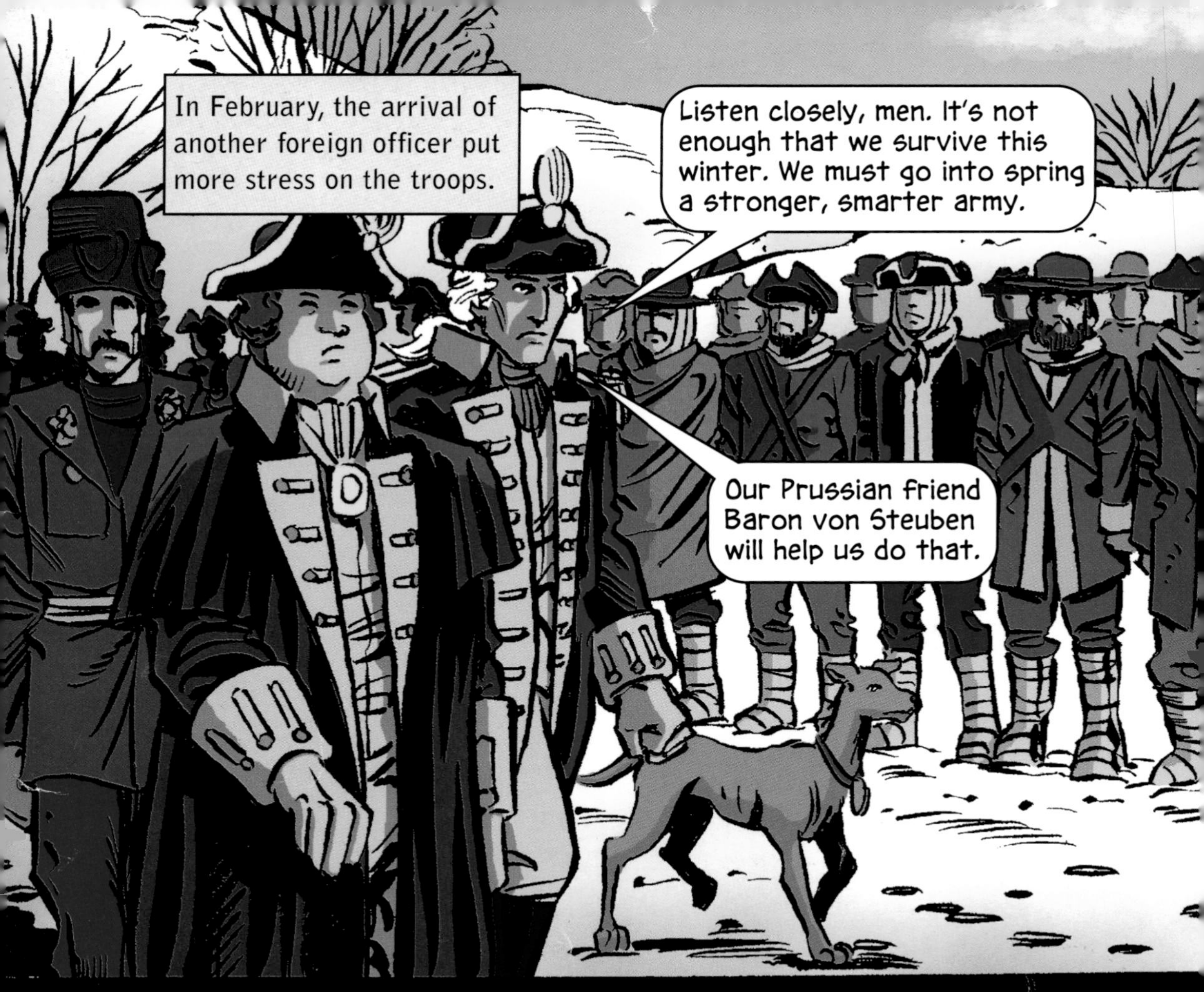
In February, the arrival of another foreign officer put more stress on the troops.
Listen closely, men. It's not enough that we survive this winter. We must go into spring a stronger, smarter army.
Our Prussian friend Baron von Steuben will help us do that.

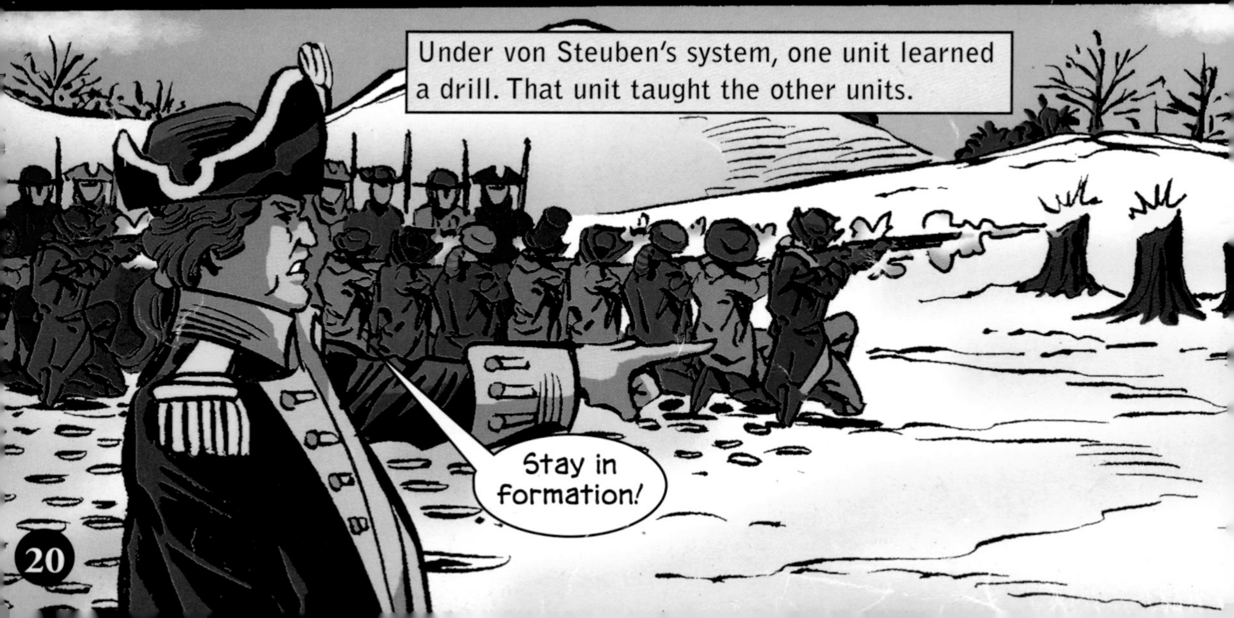
Under von Steuben's system, one unit learned a drill. That unit taught the other units.
Stay in formation!

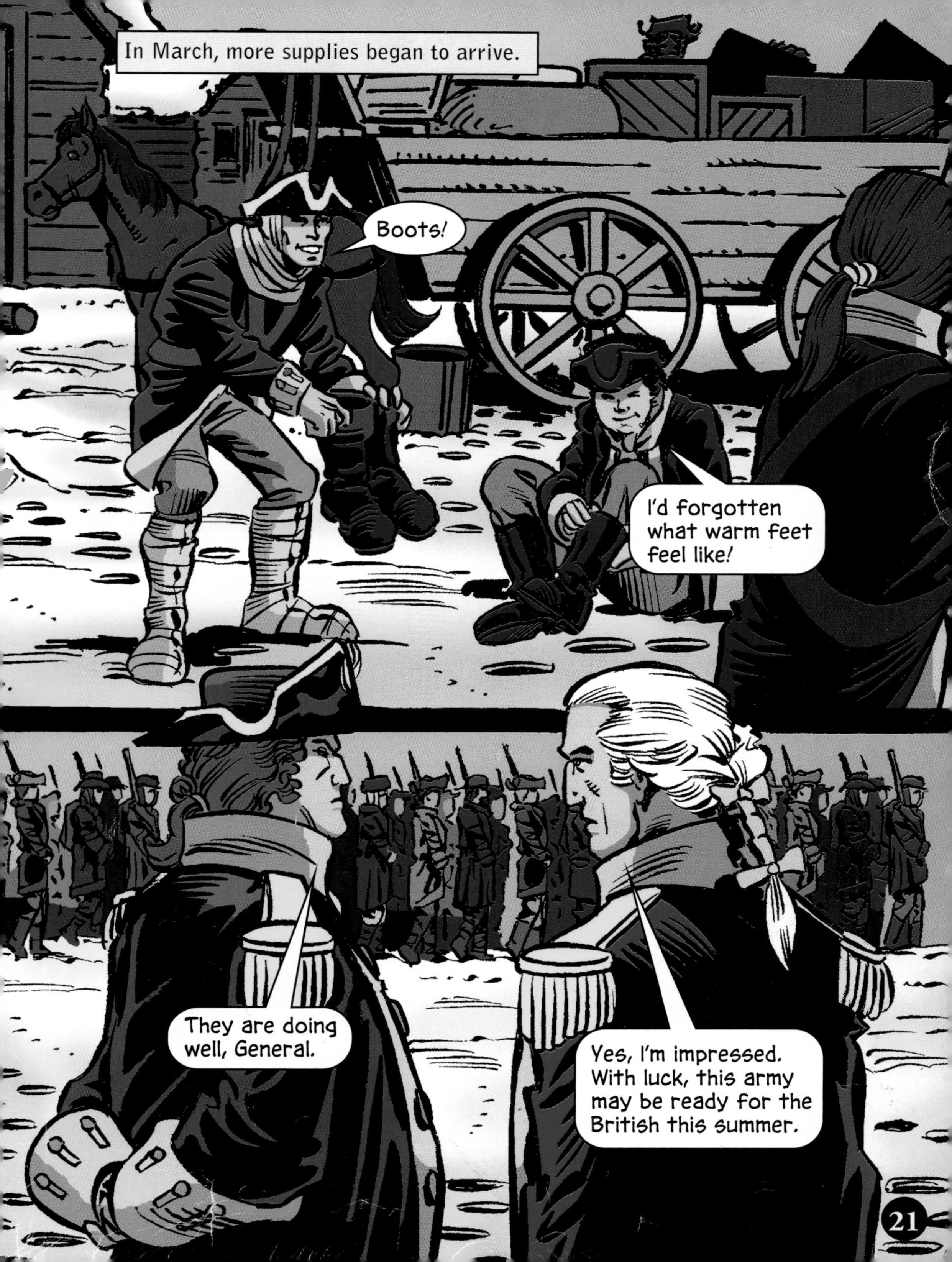
In March, more supplies began to arrive.
Boots!
I'd forgotten what warm feet feel like!
They are doing well, General.
Yes, I'm impressed. With luck, this army may be ready for the British this summer.

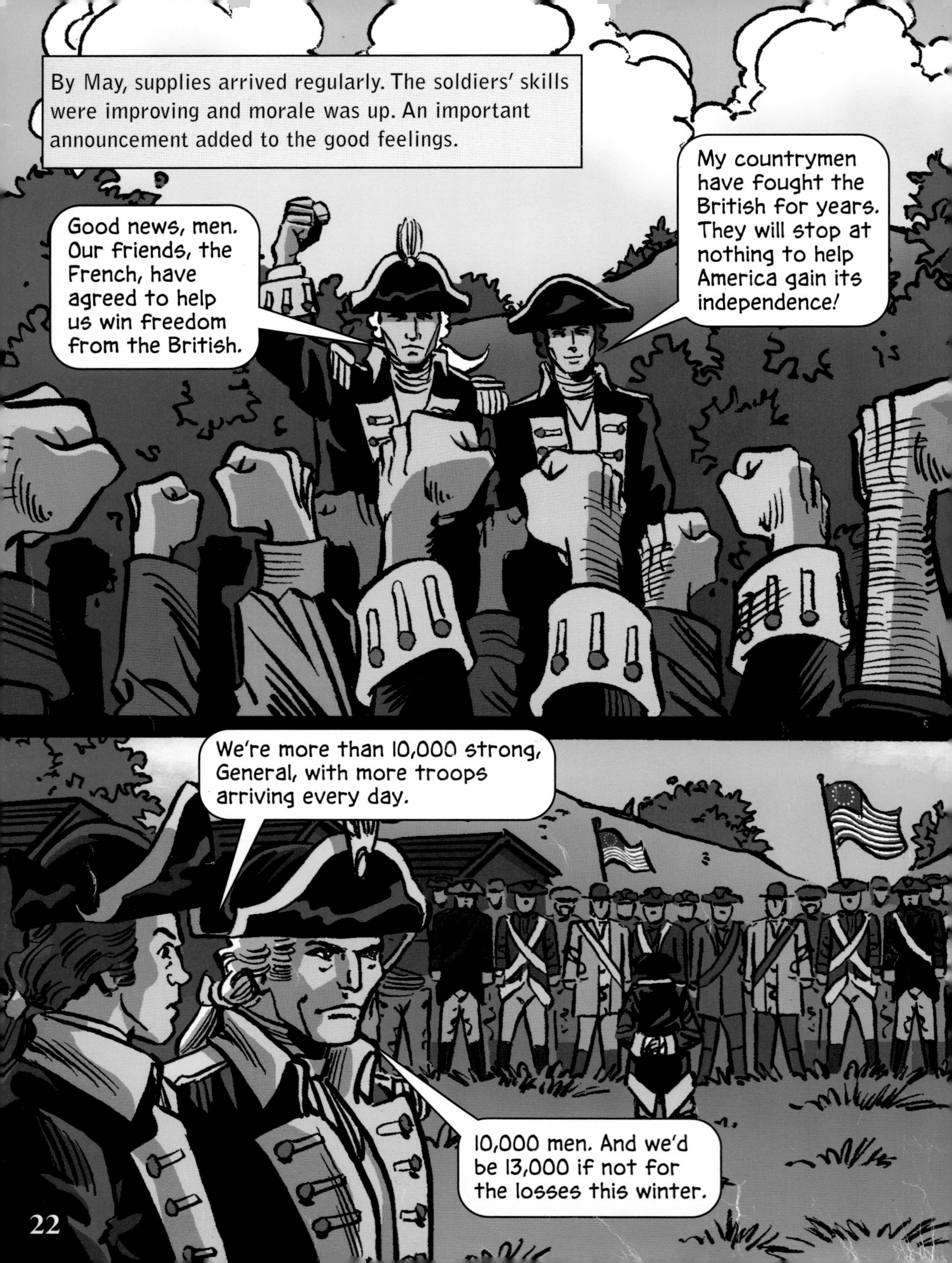

By May, supplies arrived regularly. The soldiers' skills were improving and morale was up. An important announcement added to the good feelings.
Good news, men. Our friends, the French, have agreed to help us win freedom from the British.
My countrymen have fought the British for years. They will stop at nothing to help America gain its independence!
We're more than 10,000 strong, General, with more troops arriving every day.
10,000 men. And we'd be 13,000 if not for the losses this winter.

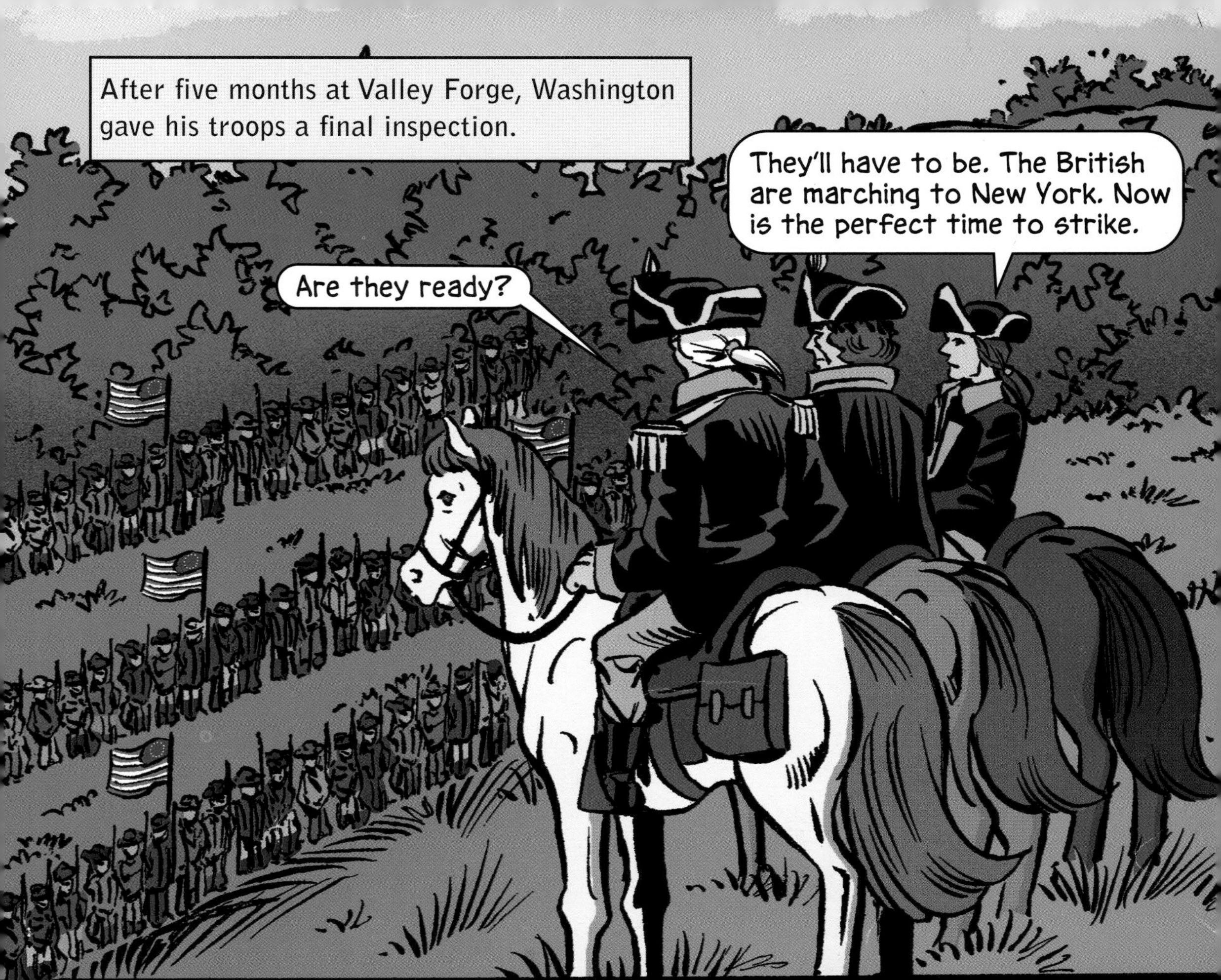
After five months at Valley Forge, Washington gave his troops a final inspection.
Are they ready?
They'll have to be. The British are marching to New York. Now is the perfect time to strike.

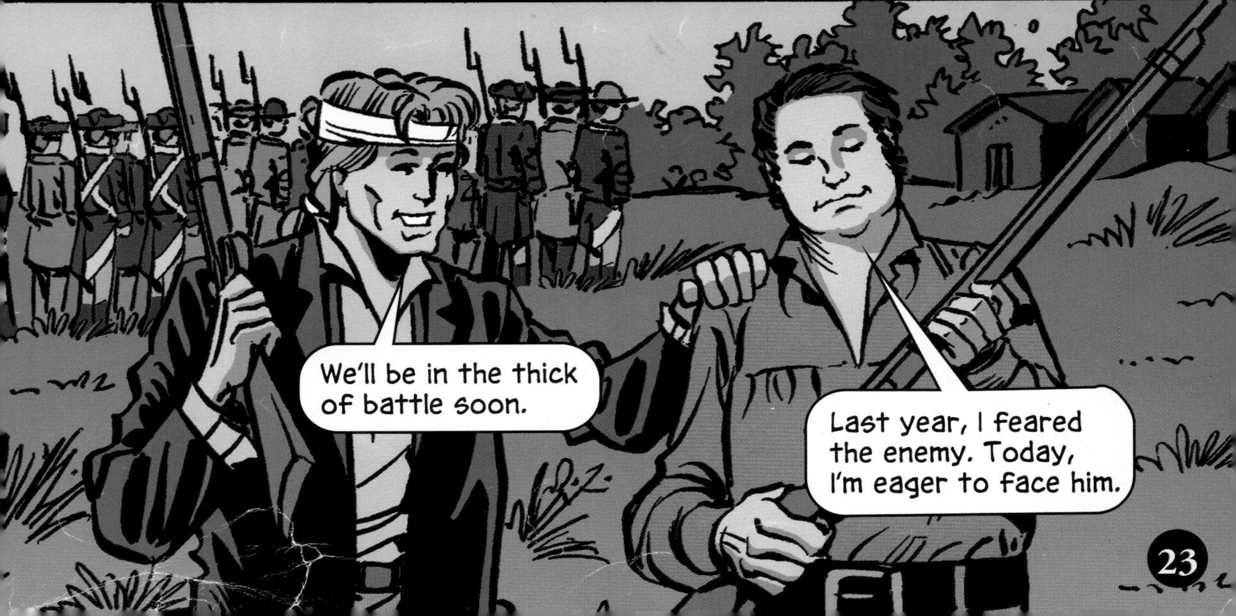
We'll be in the thick of battle soon.
Last year, I feared the enemy. Today, I'm eager to face him.

CHAPTER 4

A NEW ARMY

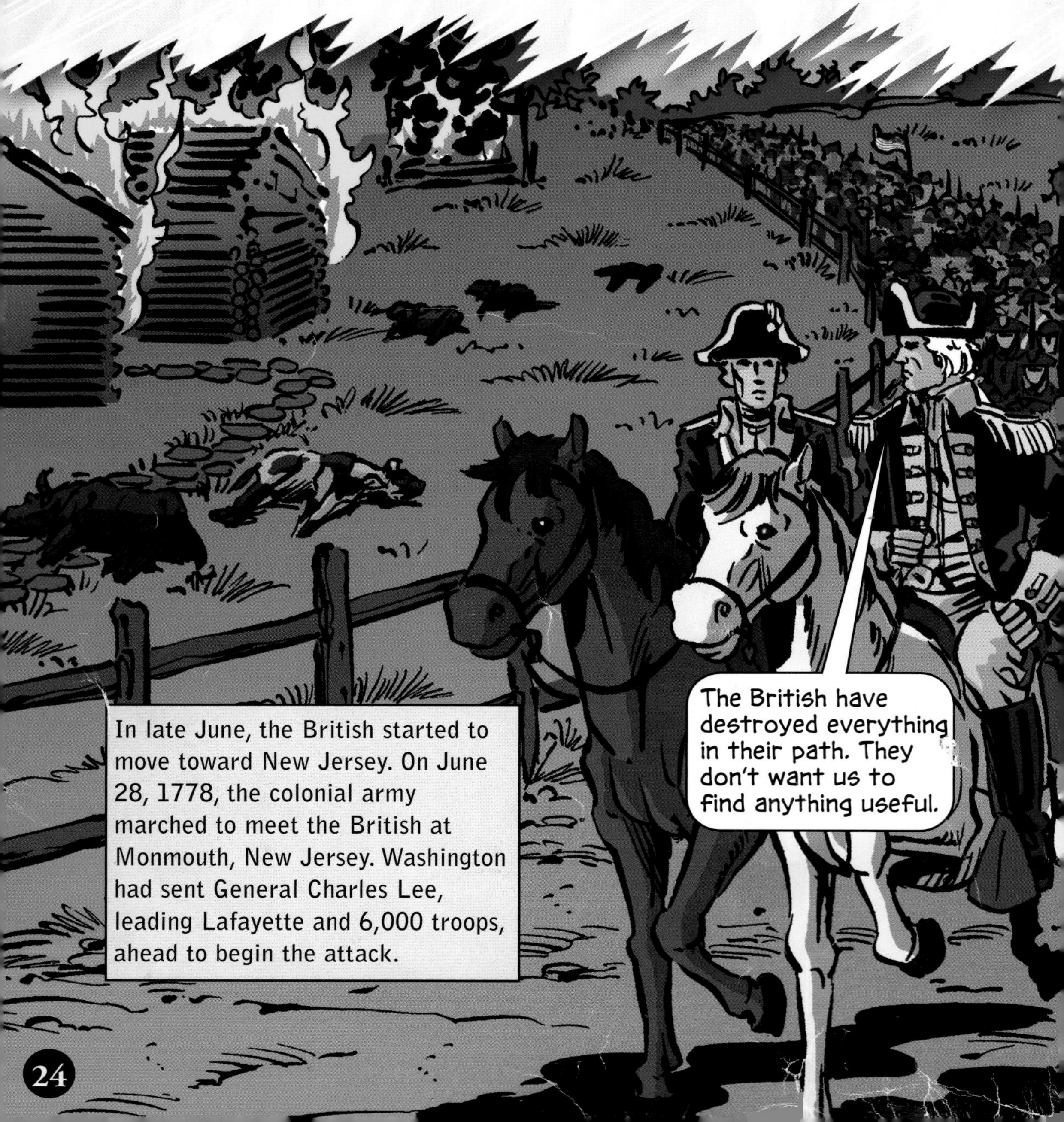
In late June, the British started to move toward New Jersey. On June 28, 1778, the colonial army marched to meet the British at Monmouth, New Jersey. Washington had sent General Charles Lee, leading Lafayette and 6,000 troops, ahead to begin the attack.
The British have destroyed everything in their path. They don't want us to find anything useful.

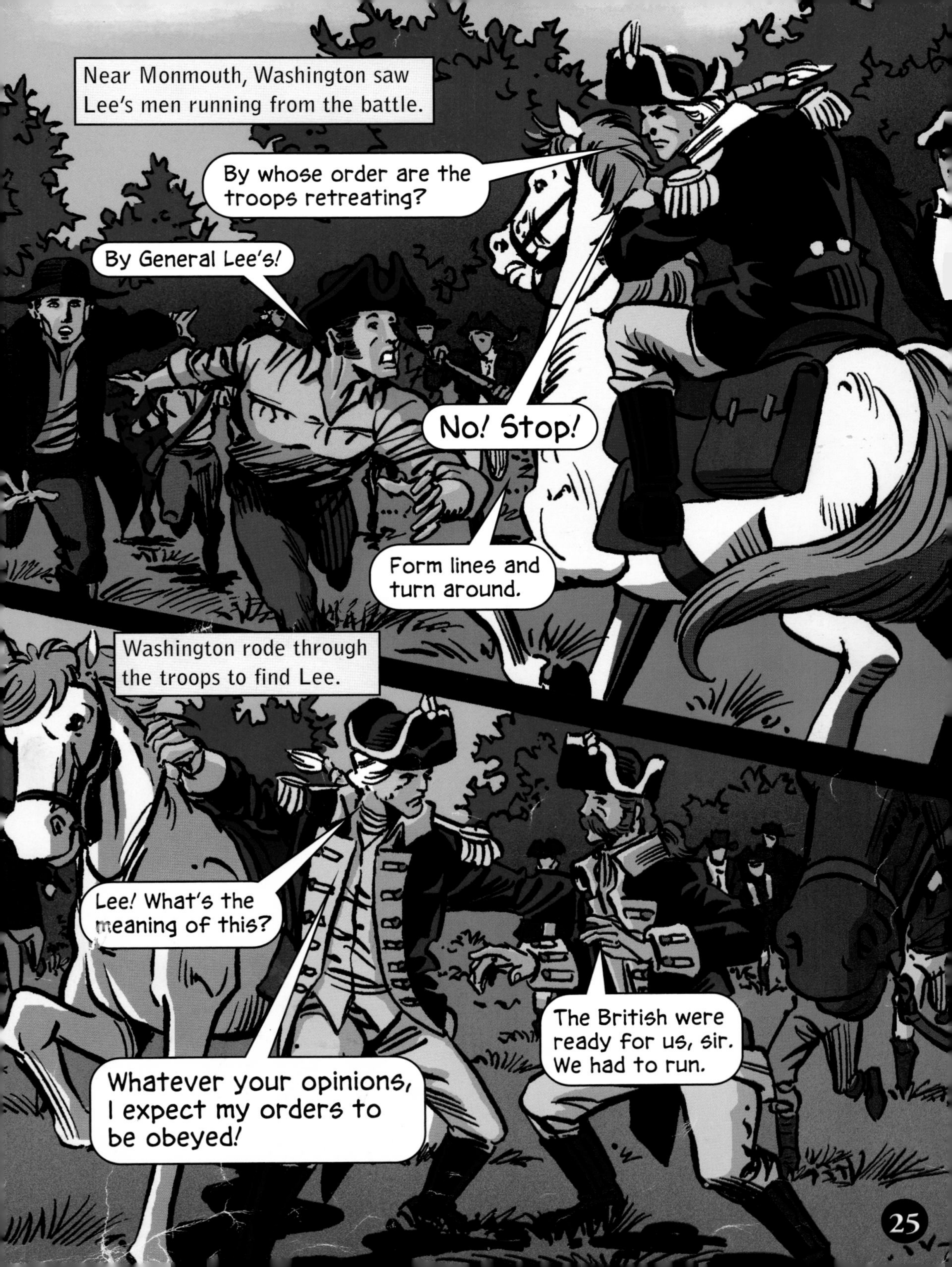
Near Monmouth, Washington saw Lee's men running from the battle.
By whose order are the troops retreating?
By General Lee's!
No! Stop!
Form lines and turn around.
Washington rode through the troops to find Lee.
Lee! What's the meaning of this?
The British were ready for us, sir. We had to run.
Whatever your opinions, I expect my orders to be obeyed!

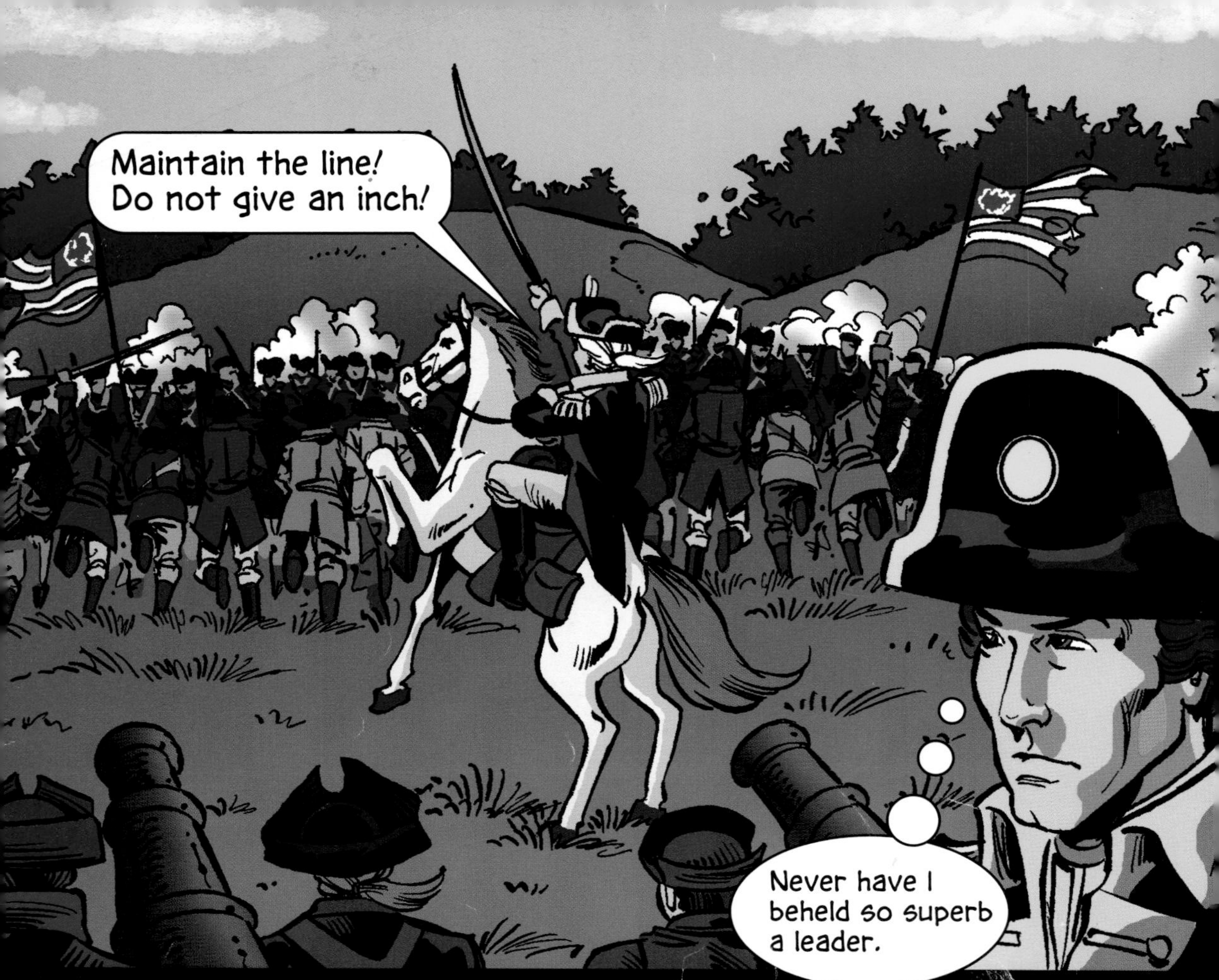
Maintain the line! Do not give an inch!
Never have I beheld so superb a leader.

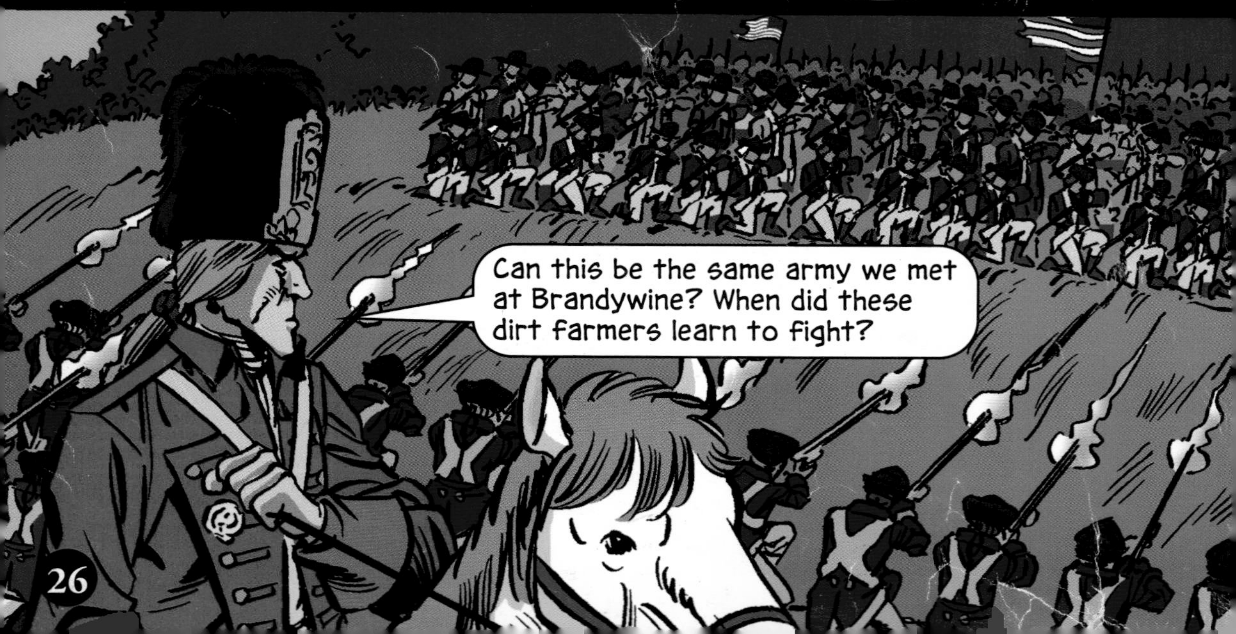
Can this be the same army we met at Brandywine? When did these dirt farmers learn to fight?

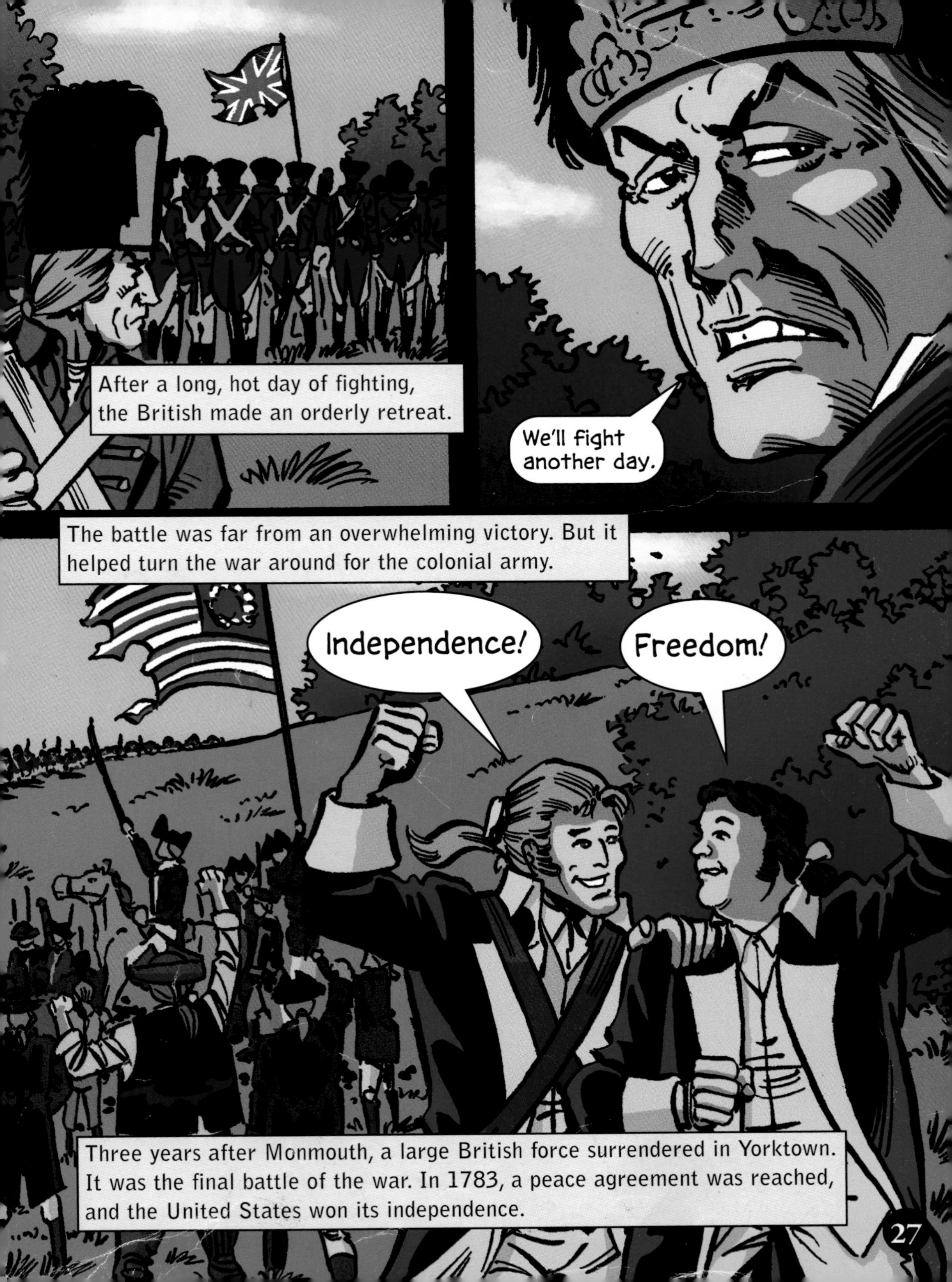
After a long, hot day of fighting, the British made an orderly retreat.
We'll fight another day.
The battle was far from an overwhelming victory. But it helped turn the war around for the colonial army.
Independence!
Freedom!
Three years after Monmouth, a large British force surrendered in Yorktown. It was the final battle of the war. In 1783, a peace agreement was reached, and the United States won its independence.

VALLEY FORGE

- Today, you can visit a national park located where the colonial army camped at Valley Forge. The house George Washington used as headquarters still stands there. Visitors can see what the soldiers' log huts looked like and learn more about how they lived.

- Many historians credit Nathanael Greene with helping the colonial army survive Valley Forge. Greene took over as the army's quartermaster in March of 1778. The quartermaster's job is to supply the army. Greene worked hard to send every bit of food and clothing he could find to the camp.

- The 3,000 men who died at or near Valley Forge were buried in unmarked graves.

- At first, Baron von Steuben had trouble training the colonial troops. He was used to troops who obeyed orders right away. He quickly learned that the American soldiers were different. It wasn't enough for him to tell troops to do something. He also had to explain to the soldiers why they should do it.

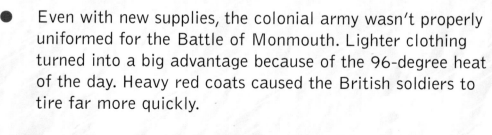

- Even with new supplies, the colonial army wasn't properly uniformed for the Battle of Monmouth. Lighter clothing turned into a big advantage because of the 96-degree heat of the day. Heavy red coats caused the British soldiers to tire far more quickly.

- The Battle of Monmouth was the last major battle fought in the Northern colonies. The rest of the major battles of the Revolutionary War were fought in the South, including the final Battle of Yorktown.

GLOSSARY

certificate (sur-TIF-uh-kit)—a government bond that promised payment at a later date for supplies

desert (di-ZURT)—to leave an army without permission

fire cake (FIRE KAYK)—a mix of flour and water baked on a hot stone

infirmary (in-FUR-mur-ee)—a place where sick people are cared for

lash (LASH)—a stroke with a whip

typhus (TYE-fus)—a disease that causes a high fever and diarrhea

tyranny (TIHR-uh-nee)—unjust rule by a government

INTERNET SITES

FactHound offers a safe, fun way to find Internet sites related to this book. All of the sites on FactHound have been researched by our staff.

Here's how:

1. Visit *www.facthound.com*.
2. Type in this special code **0736849750** for age-appropriate sites. Or enter a search word related to this book for a more general search.
3. Click on the **Fetch It** button.

FactHound will fetch the best sites for you!

READ MORE

Ammon, Richard. *Valley Forge.* New York: Holiday House, 2004.

Dell, Pamela. *The Doctor's Boy: A Story about Valley Forge in the Winter of 1777–1778.* Scrapbooks of America. Maple Plain, Minn.: Tradition Books, 2004.

Doeden, Matt. *George Washington: Leading a New Nation.* Graphic Library. Graphic Biographies. Mankato, Minn.: Capstone Press, 2006.

Murray, Aaron R. (editor). *American Revolution: Battles and Leaders.* New York: DK Pub., 2004.

BIBLIOGRAPHY

Brookhiser, Richard. *Founding Father: Rediscovering George Washington.* New York: The Free Press, 1996.

Fleming, Thomas. *Liberty! The American Revolution.* New York: Viking, 1997.

Marrin, Albert. *The War for Independence: The Story of the American Revolution.* New York: Atheneum, 1988.

Tebbel, John. *Turning the World Upside Down: Inside the American Revolution.* New York: Orion Books, 1993.

INDEX